THE INTENSIVE GROUP EXPERIENCE
The New Pietism

BOOKS BY THOMAS C. ODEN
Published by The Westminster Press

The Intensive Group Experience:
The New Pietism

Beyond Revolution: A Response
to the Underground Church

Contemporary Theology
and Psychotherapy

Kerygma and Counseling

Radical Obedience:
The Ethics of Rudolf Bultmann

THE INTENSIVE
GROUP EXPERIENCE

The New Pietism

by THOMAS C. ODEN

THE WESTMINSTER PRESS
Philadelphia

ISBN 0-664-20933-5 (cloth)

ISBN 0-664-24951-5 (paper)

Library of Congress Catalog Card No. 75-182539

BOOK DESIGN BY
DOROTHY ALDEN SMITH

Published by The Westminster Press ®
Philadelphia, Pennsylvania

PRINTED IN THE UNITED STATES OF AMERICA

For my own intensive group

Edrita, Clark, Edward, and Laura

with love and affection

Contents

Preface   11

Introduction
THE ENCOUNTER CULTURE   17

Chapter One
A REPERTOIRE OF INTENSIVE
GROUP STRATEGIES   29

    1. Distance and Closeness   31

    2. Body Space and Control   43

    3. Life Cycle Fantasy   48

Chapter Two
THE NEW PIETISM   56

    1. The Tradition Against Tradition   56

    2. The Demythologizing of Pietistic Encounter   60

    3. Comparison of the Pietistic Encounter Styles
       with Current Encounter   69

    4. The Soft Revolution: Then and Now   77

    5. The Medium (Group Encounter)
       Is the Massage   85

Chapter Three
GROUP TRUST AND ULTIMATE TRUST   89

   1. The Implicit Ontological Assumptions of
      Group Trust   90

   2. Nonverbal Communication and a Theology
      of Happenings   98

   3. The Structure of Encounter Theology   103

   4. The Incredible Boredom of Theology in the
      Presence of the Encounter Culture   112

Chapter Four
INCONSISTENCIES AND
MISCALCULATIONS OF THE
MOVEMENT   118

   1. Phoniness, Brevity, and Anti-intellectualism   119

   2. Permissiveness, Psychedelics,
      and Sensationalism   124

   3. Some Philosophical and Moral Issues   130

Chapter Five
ENCOUNTER AND CELEBRATION   140

   1. Guidelines and Hazards for Transverbal
      Experimentation in Worship   141

   2. Body Language in Liturgical Innovation   146

   3. The Demand for Risk-Taking   151

   4. Youth Culture and Encounter Culture   162

Notes   169

Preface

One of the fastest growing social phenomena in our time is the encounter group. In a mobile society with a deep hunger for intimacy, the intensive group experience has provided a means by which persons can experience significant encounters that seem to be denied them in routine social exchanges. With accelerating mobility and historical change, it is imperative that our society develop social processes for achieving genuine intimacy. The encounter culture represents such an experimental effort which may have great significance for the church. However, at this time it needs serious and thoughtful criticism more than it needs a new batch of devotees.

To whom is this book addressed? (*a*) To persons nurtured in the Judeo-Christian tradition who have not experienced growth groups, marathons, intensive encounter groups, or experiments in nonverbal communication, but who want to learn something about them and to explore their possible usefulness for the religious community and the shaping of the spiritual life. (*b*) To persons nurtured in the Judeo-Christian tradition who may have participated in the intensive group experience in profoundly moving ways but who have not yet learned to assess how that experience relates to their understanding of community, intimacy, self-disclosure, honesty, and love, and yet who suspect that there are important links and wish to see them made. (*c*) To persons whose lives have been profoundly shaped by the intensive group experience but do not think of themselves or these processes in religious categories, who nonetheless would like to see traditional theology take the intensive group processes seriously and critically in order to clarify their religious promise.

After an introduction to "The Encounter Culture," we present "A Repertoire of Intensive Group Strategies" (Chapter One), each one of which is given a brief critical assessment with respect to its possibilities and limitations for spiritual formation. The purpose of this chapter is (*a*) to introduce persons who are unfamiliar with these processes to an elementary repertoire of intensive group strategies; (*b*) to select those group experiences which have the most promise for being reshaped for use in experimental worship and religious education and to describe them carefully; and (*c*) to apply some basic theological insights to their interpretation and critique. This chapter will describe group experiences designed to deepen *intrapersonal* awareness, group processes that focus on *interpersonal* communication, and group processes that aim toward *transpersonal* awareness.

Our principal historical thesis is that the antecedents of the current encounter group processes are to be found chiefly in the life and literature of Protestant and Jewish pietism. Stated differently, the encounter group is a demythologized and secularized form of a style of interpersonal encounter and community that is familiar to historians of Protestant pietism (and also of the Jewish

hasidic movement which was parallel to it). It emphasized "here and now" experiencing, intensive small-group
encounter, honest confession amid a trusting community,
experimental mysticism, mutual pastoral care, and the
operation of the Spirit at the level of nonverbal communication. Chapter Two, "The New Pietism," clarifies
and develops this thesis. Its purpose is to show in a
plausible way to group process participants that their
work exists in a continuing historic tradition of which
they have generally been unaware. Most of the persons
involved in the movement have not been trained to think
historically, so this is a service that needs to be rendered
by those in touch with the tradition; but it must be
rendered in a way that can be made thoroughly credible
even to those who had imagined they were doing something entirely unprecedented.

Chapter Three, "Group Trust and Ultimate Trust,"
explores the hidden kinship between high trust levels
in small groups and the dynamics of trust in Judeo-
Christian thought. We are searching for analogies between the threefold structure of worship and theology
and the threefold sequence of encounter group change.
We will look for the similarities and differences between
the implicit theology operating in growing groups and
the explicit "good news" of the Christian community. We
will probe the analogies between human trust and the
trustworthiness of God. We will show how the issues of
nonverbal communication are deeply woven into the
Biblical witness to God's incarnate happening love. We
will ask whether the next major task of theology might
be the possibility of a nonverbal theology. Although
this chapter may seem to be more specifically addressed
to religious educators, I hope to make its argument

plausible to those who do not think of themselves as being interested directly in theology.

Then we will analyze some of the "Inconsistencies and Miscalculations of the Movement" (Chapter Four). Seeking to avoid the polemic and caricature that have characterized the popular literature on encounter groups, I offer the circumspect reader a series of modest criticisms of the human potential movement, probing its temptations to antinomianism, anti-intellectualism, oversimplification of the human quandary, and introversion, while remaining appreciative of its basic intent.

Our study will come to a practical focus in the final chapter, "Encounter and Celebration," with the straightforward question: What do religious communities have to learn from encounter groups? Should the church become a growth center? In the light of their historic kinship, how can the present alienation between existing religious communities and experimental encounter groups be overcome? What can be appropriated and what must be transmuted? How can this knowledge be applied in liturgical experimentation? What in particular can we learn from experiments in nonverbal communication that might help us to reshape our understanding of the worshiping community?

Among the many persons to whom I owe special thanks for insights or encouragement without which this effort would not have been completed are National Training Laboratories Fellows Kenneth Benne, Racine Brown, Shepherd Insel, and Sherman Kingsbury; Esalen's Bernard Gunther and William Schutz; transactional analysts Thomas Harris and John Hoff; Stuart Gilbreath of the Center for Studies of the Person; and family counselors Don Williamson and Don Young, with each of whom I have shared significant group training or co-training laboratories or clinical experiences. To Daniel Joyce and Thompson Shannon I am grateful for enabling a sabbatical leave from Phillips Seminary in 1970 in order to study the intensive group process at Houston's Institute of Religion, the Texas Medical Center, and the VA Hospital's Human Relations Laboratory under the imaginative direction of Phil Hanson and Walter M. O'Connell. My Drew University colleagues Will Herberg, Bard Thompson, Nelson Thayer, Russell Richey, and Kenneth Rowe have shared in the development of the historical analysis I shall present. Above all, I am grateful for my students, or co-learners as I would prefer to view them, at Phillips, Houston, and Drew, who have contributed so much to my own growth both personally and professionally by giving me constructive, well-targeted feedback about myself as their teacher and fellow human being.

T.C.O.

Drew University Graduate School
Madison, New Jersey

Introduction

THE ENCOUNTER CULTURE

This book began as an irrepressible intuition that dawned upon me as I worked with encounter groups as an extension of my previous study of psychotherapy. As I listened to and shared in a wide variety of group processes, both as a participant and as a facilitator, I began to feel that there was something about all this that I had heard before. Even though its language was "mod" and its spirit venturesome, my intuition told me that this was a repetition of a model that was somehow deeply written into the Western experience. Then it dawned on me that what was happening was a reappropriation of the style of small-group encounter which was a vast popular movement beginning in the seventeenth century called pietism.

The more I explored my initial intuition, the more it proved itself to be accurate. This discussion is the result of five years of accelerating immersion in the "movement" of small-group encounter, and an attempt to come into a critical and realistic dialogue with it as a Protestant theologian.

There are many varieties of encounter groups. Some are designed for business executives, some for black-white encounter or for intergenerational dialogue, others for couples, religious groups, or students. There are also many different methods—Gestalt techniques,[1] bioenergetics,[2] laboratory learning,[3] psychodrama,[4] etc. They go by many names—growth groups, basic encounter groups, open encounter groups, transactional analysis groups, T-groups, sensory awareness groups, etc.[5] But in the midst of all these differences, they have at least one feature in common: they are all dealing with the *intensive group experience*, utilizing the small group as the medium of interpersonal and personal growth, improved communication, and constructive behavioral change.[6]

Sessions may range in time from brief three-hour "microlabs" to intensive thirty-six-hour marathons, from weekend workshops to three-week intensive vocational retooling laboratories, from groups that will meet only for several hours to groups that will meet for many weeks.

The educators, psychologists, and social scientists who are leading these groups are increasingly careful not to make any therapeutic claims for them. Their avowed intent is not to do therapy but to increase the quality and the clarity of human communication. The hoped-for result is improved learning about oneself, not psychotherapeutic healing (although there may be some so-called "therapeutic" consequences). They have borrowed a rich mix of techniques and resources from group dynamics, behavioral psychology, human relations training, social psychology, leadership training, group therapy, meditation, psychodrama, and theater games, in order to "turn people on" to each other and to their own feeling processes. They are not trying to make sick people well, so much as to make well people better.[7]

The layman who knows nothing of encounter groups, T-groups, marathons, sensory awareness, etc., surely has been isolated from the main currents of American religious life of the past decade. With increasing acceleration in the last five years, the encounter culture has spread from town to town, retreat center to retreat center, and church to church, with such power (some would compare it to a terminal stage of malignancy) that it is impossible to ignore it as a force in religious life, regardless of how one might evaluate it. Literally thousands of religious educators, pastors, laymen, and youth have been introduced in one form or another to encounter groups.[8] Some laymen have met the encounter group techniques through their business training, whereas others have experienced it through educational, civic, governmental, religious, or health-care channels, but almost no one has been left untouched by it in some way.

Although official sponsorship of this movement is difficult to specify, since it has come largely from non-Establishment sources, it is at least possible to point to such groups as the National Educational Association's National Training Laboratories,[9] The American Association of Humanistic Psychology,[10] and the Institute for Transactional Analysis,[11] as clearinghouses for the movement.

Advocates claim that these groups already are performing important corrective functions in our society, cutting through dishonesty, helping persons to develop better sensory contact with the world, deepening the capacity for joy, and improving feedback procedures. The movement also has its share of critics, who view the encounter culture as dangerous, irresponsible, fanatical, faddish, exhibitionist, and counter-productive.[12]

Sam Keen has used the term "soft revolution" to describe the "new secular religion" that has been emerging during the 1960's—"eclectic, experiential, mystical and nonprofessional—a do-it-yourself kit composed of disciplines and insights drawn from many religious and occult traditions." [13]

"We are in the middle of two revolutions," says Keen. "One is *hard*, explosive and political. It is concerned primarily with the redistribution of political power and is committed to a strategy of direct confrontation. The other is *soft*, implosive and religious. It is concerned primarily with the alteration of consciousness, with erotic and mystical experience and with the resacralization of intimate relationships. The hard revolution finds its focus in the emergence of power groups—black, brown, student. The soft revolution is diffuse and without organizational manifestations, but its visible outposts are the 'growth centers' (now numbering between 90 and 100) which have been modeled on the Esalen Institute." [14]

To many churchmen, such things as sensory awareness, body affirmation, emphasis on tactility, and sensitivity training sound like something quite alien to the Christian life, and in fact perhaps quite dangerous. Other churchmen who have actually been involved with these groups often testify to a deepening of their religious sensitivities and experiences, and to a hope that these processes might quicken the spirit of religious communities in our time. By far, most of the persons (studies show 90 to 98 percent) who have participated in encounter groups have indicated that they felt they benefited from the experience.[15]

Persons who have not experienced basic group encounter may be wondering what we mean when we speak of "intensive group experiencing." The most concise statement of what happens in such groups has been made by Carl Rogers, who described in fifteen stages some *personal interactions that frequently take place in encounter groups*.[16] Since these correspond with my own observations, I will summarize them, hoping it will serve both as an introduction to basic group encounter for those who need it and as a refresher for those who have been deeply involved in it:

1. Most groups begin with a period of polite surface interaction, some awkwardness, often frustration and confusion combined with bewilderment about who is in charge.

2. Persons show their public selves, or masks, while their private selves remain cautiously withdrawn. They wonder if the group can be trusted. There is a general resistance in the group to expression of feelings, and a reliance on ritual behaviors.

3. Some past feelings may be cautiously expressed or described.

4. Negative feelings are expressed, often past-oriented. Some current personal feelings may also be expressed at this stage. Often this takes the form of attacking the facilitator for not giving the kind of guidance that was expected. This is the point when persons begin to ask and find out whether this is a place where "here and now" negative feelings can be expressed without disastrous results, and how they are dealt with.

5. If negative feelings can be negotiated, the group moves on to the exploration of personally meaningful materials. There is an increasing realization that the group is "our group," and that we can make of it what we wish.

6. "Here and now" feelings toward others in the

group, both positive and negative, are more fully expressed.

7. In response to these expressions, group members often show a remarkable spontaneous capacity for dealing helpfully and constructively with the pain and suffering of others. "This kind of ability shows up so commonly in groups," remarks Rogers, "that it has led me to feel that the ability to be healing or therapeutic is far more common in human life than we suppose. Often it needs only the permission granted—or freedom made possible —by the climate of a free flowing group experience to become evident."

8. Increased self-acceptance ensues—the sense that it is all right to be me, to feel my feelings.

9. This is often followed by the cracking of facades and impatience with defenses. During this phase, the group may make it difficult for some of its members to continue to live behind masks. "Gently at times, almost savagely at others, the group *demands* that the individual be himself, that his current feelings not be hidden, that he remove the mask of ordinary social intercourse."

10. Feedback is received from others. One learns how one appears to others.

11. Confrontation occurs. Painful or difficult conflicts with others are expressed and renegotiated.

12. The helping relationship continues outside the group sessions, with group members often giving of themselves deeply to assist each other.

13. Rogers uses the term "basic encounter" to describe the matured stage of group encounter where persons feel completely with and for the others, where negative feelings are fully expressed and embraced by deeper feelings of acceptance. Persons experience each other in "I-thou"

relationships, or relationships where persons are fully prized as persons and not treated as things or objects.

14. The expression of positive feelings and closeness to others is thus made possible in a new way.

15. Positive behavioral changes result from these interactions.

I prefer the term "intensive group experience" to such terms as "growth group," "T-group," or "therapy group." What is an intensive group? A group of human beings who exist in dialogue and encounter, often within a limited time span, and at a level of emotive depth in personal transactions.[17]

What is *encounter?* Leveling and confrontation. Leveling involves my telling you how I am experiencing myself. Confrontation involves my telling you how you are coming across to me, especially in its more painful negative forms.

What is *dialogue?* Self-disclosure and listening. Self-disclosure occurs when I reveal to you how I am feeling, who I am, how I came to be this way. Listening occurs when I hear your self-disclosure.

Thus "intensive group experience" is an umbrella term for a diverse set of phenomena. The term serves us well precisely because it provides an overarching description of several different types of groups, including personal growth groups, laboratory learning or T-groups, open encounter groups, and certain religious groups.

One way to probe more deeply into the concept of the intensive group experience is to inquire where these words came from.

1. *Intensive,* from the Latin *intendere* (to stretch out or draw taut), refers to an activity or process that is

heightened, compacted, focused, and purposively augmented. It demands attention and concentration. As in
colors or lighting with greater intensity, if a group is intensive, it has more action moving within it, more radi-
ance or brilliance; more heat is generated. The more intense a group is, the more vivid, poignant, passionate,
sharp, acute, will be its feeling contents and interpersonal exchanges.

2. *Group* merely refers to persons or things assembled
in an identifiable relationship with a certain degree of
similarity. The English word comes from French and
Teutonic words similar to our word "crop." Persons in an
intensive group, therefore, would be persons coming together with compacted effect upon each other, with an
augmentation of their interpersonal exchanges both in
quantity and quality.

3. To *experience* something, from the Latin *experiri*
(to put to the test), is to try something out, or put it to
the test of one's sensory faculties and reasoning. Experience is personal knowledge, or knowledge that has been
run through one's own personal history and understanding. We speak of a person as being "experienced" when
he has accumulated a great fund of experiences, or found
himself immersed in many learning contexts in which he
has learned a great deal. Thus a group experience is a
learning context in which one tries out his feelings in
the presence of others, or tests out what it means to be
himself in the presence of others. A group experience involves a collection of people who come together in an
identifiable way in order to experience each other more
fully and to learn from their impact upon each other. An
intensive group experience thus would be a context
where such impacts are intensified and augmented, and

the learnings compacted in a brief time span.[18]

Equally important in the vocabulary of this discussion is the word *encounter,* from the French *encontrer* (to meet face-to-face). This word often has the connotation of conflict, but it also may, significantly enough, have the connotation of intimacy. Encounters often are conflicted, yet often have within them the possibility of greater intimacy.

Much of what we are describing in this variegated movement may be summarized under the term "encounter culture," which we borrow from William Schutz's *Here Comes Everybody,* subtitled "Bodymind and Encounter Culture." [19] The term "encounter culture" deserves clarification, since it is a rather diffuse term but one that we find extremely valuable in developing our proposal. "Encounter culture" refers to the special subculture that has emerged in and around the human potential movement and human relations training groups, with their growth centers, sensory awareness exercises, and encounter life-style. Schutz employs the term "encounter culture" in contrast to the idea of a "counter culture," not merely as a play on words but also as a description of two substantially different (although in some ways similar) alternatives for radical change in our society.

The *counter* culture has been widely described as a "great negation" (Marcuse) of the fundamental institutions of the West, of sexual repressiveness, and of the war machine which manifests the worst aspects of advanced industrial society.[20] Its critique of society is strongly political, although it is not limited to the political. Its exponents and exemplars are typically involved in radical political dissent and quasi-revolutionary activity.

Its heroes are Marcuse, Che Guevara, the Panthers, Fanon, Hayden, Rubin, Hoffman, and others.

Political activism is not a characteristic of the *encounter* culture, nor is political rhetoric. Rather, it is a diffuse consciousness-changing movement that is closely associated with the life-style of encounter groups and experiments in rapid behavioral change through intensive group processes. The encounter culture manifests many of the aspects that Charles Reich describes as Consciousness III, although that term is fraught with unfortunate oversimplifications and deserves the stringent criticism it has received.[21]

Many persons today are asking themselves about the potential worthwhileness of encounter groups: Should I become involved in a growth center or encounter context where these kinds of experiences are being programmed? This discussion is in part designed to answer that question and not to answer simply yes or no but to try to clarify for the Christian lay reader what at least one theologian sees as the promise and the limitations of groups such as these. Criticisms of the movement are focused in Chapter Four. However, I evaluate positively much that is happening in the movement as a whole. For most people, with the exception of those with deep pathological psychic conflicts, these groups will be helpful. What is more, people in the Judeo-Christian community who have been nurtured with the language and understandings of the Biblical witness can make significant contributions to these groups. They celebrate the infinite forgiving love of God which group encounter may know only in an indirect and incognito fashion. However, I am also convinced that many of the hangups which traditionalist Christians bring to involvements

of this kind will make the dialogue difficult. I am refer-
ring especially to our reticence about body language
enfleshing our feelings, especially aggressive, hostile, and
intimate ones. These are problems which will have to be
worked through. Part of my motivation for writing this
book is that I think many people are just at the point
of considering whether it is possible to work through all
these issues and at the same time be faithful to the Christian tradition; or whether the human potential movement
is something that has to go on completely apart from or
over against the Christian community.

Christianity and the encounter culture deserve to be in
serious dialogue. This does not mean that the church
should become a "growth center," although in some cases
that needs to be tried experimentally. Nor does it mean
that the encounter process should become saturated with
overt traditional religious imagery. Let it be what it is
as a secularized movement, relating realistically to where
people are. But its secularizing momentum deserves to
be in a richer dialogue with the wisdom of the Christian
tradition that spawned it.

Our question is: To what degree does the rapidly
spreading movement of group encounter lend itself to
accommodation to the Judeo-Christian tradition, and to
practical utilization in the reshaping of worship, corporate life, adult education, pastoral care, and spiritual
formation?

Chapter One

A REPERTOIRE
OF INTENSIVE GROUP STRATEGIES

We will begin by describing a variety of experiments in interpersonal transaction that can be done with young people or adults within the framework of religious education and experimental worship. Although this is not a "how to do it" book, this section is designed to clarify to the reader who has not been involved in these processes something of their scope, dynamics, and interpretation. We hope it will stimulate pastors, religious educators, and others into searching for new forms of intensive group experiencing appropriate to their local situations. Our purpose is not to provide an exhaustive compendium of these group strategies, but merely to introduce the reader to a selected number of them.

One warning: There is a curious sense of abstractness about describing these processes in skeletal fashion, whereas if they are experienced in a group, they quickly come to life and one feels the sense of having participated in a live happening. If there may understandably be something sterile in reading about these processes, there is something much more exciting about participating in them. So the bare-bones description may seem dull and perhaps a little phony. Even if we were to supply verbatim reports of group transactions, I do not think such reports would provide the kind of vitality that would be experienced in one's own group.

These are experiments which would be appropriate in almost any church group. Of course the group leader would have to make some circumspect decisions about when they would be more or less appropriate. Some notes are included on the fitting context in each case. The optimum size of groups using these processes is six to twelve persons. Groups of more than fourteen persons are well advised to divide into two parts.

It seems desirable at this point to anticipate an objection. What we are describing here are group exercises, or, more simply, group games. These may not eventuate in any intensive group experience. Nothing guarantees that. Some people might say that we are talking, not about a sustained intensive group experience, but only of some things that groups can do when they get together. Quite candidly, this is the case. It is difficult to manipulate or control or even design an intensive group experience. I am simply describing some of the exercises that are used to develop the kinds of consciousness and trust levels in groups which make intensive group experiencing possible. I certainly do not wish to oversell such exercises, but I do think we have much to learn from them and good reason to be hopeful about applying them to religious education.

How, then, do we move from the group exercise to the group experience? Although a very important question, it cannot be answered in a formal or generalized way, since every group is unique. Everything depends upon the imagination, levels of awareness, and facilitative skills of the group leader and the persons in the group.

When we speak of a "repertoire" of intensive group strategies we are speaking of processes that have been designed to bring groups into otherwise difficult interactions in a short time span. To use the term "repertoire," however, may give the impression that one is putting on a performance, and for that reason may not be as descriptive as might be desired. A repertoire is a collection of resources. We are presenting a basic collection of operations and resources that groups can utilize to bring them closer together and to elicit intensive transactions in a brief time span.

1. DISTANCE AND CLOSENESS

Free Placement

There are times when a group will be struggling with issues of interpersonal distance.[1] Persons are wondering how close or how far they are from others. Some wish to be approached; others would prefer the safety of distance. When such feelings are being experienced by a group, the group is invited to stand up and nonverbally enact these feelings of distance with their bodies: "Vote with your feet about the distance you prefer with each person in the room. Each person may choose any distance from others that feels most comfortable. Quietly, without any talking, choose a space in the room that feels right to you. If there is someone you want to be close to or someone else you feel at a distance from, choose the space that expresses where you now are. If you want to move, move wherever you want to move." Then after the group members have moved to the place each wants to be, they may sit down and discuss how they feel about where they are, and why they chose that space. How does that space express who each person is at that moment?

Theological issues implicit in this experience are: What does your spacing of yourself say to you about your basic need for others or need for distance from others? Are you now wishing for solitude more than for intimacy? What is your body saying to you about that need? How is this distancing experience a basic expression of what Buber calls "the inter-human"? How is it a way of stating nonverbally what goes on between persons?

In what sense is your distance from other persons an expression of the way in which you see yourself in covenant with them or not in covenant with them? How does the space which you freely chose to occupy express something of your understanding of God's gift of creation? How would you choose to use this space God gives if you could choose freely here and now? (In what sense are we acknowledging our space together as a loan or claim of God, and how does our spacing of ourselves from our neighbor reflect our understanding of that loan or claim? How does our being at a distance from others express the human condition of estrangement from the neighbor and in what sense is that an expression of our estrangement from God?)

Dissonant Harmony

There are times when everyone in a group seems to be going his own way. When there is no group topic, no particular subject pursued consistently, the group might be asked to stand up in a circle with arms around each other's shoulders. Then they are to close their eyes and begin to hum. The only rule is that they cannot hum a tune that is familiar. They can hum as loud or as soft for as long as they want, or join in unison with each other— they can follow or lead if they want to. What usually develops in a situation of this sort is a "group sound" that has a strange sort of beauty of its own in the various tunes that are hummed independently. If this does happen, the group may talk about how it sounded and about the fact that disparate tunes hummed independently have a kind of harmony of their own. This is sometimes an interesting way to keep a group from becoming highly fragmented.

If the group wants to discuss this in another context, someone might ask: In what sense is our humming like history—like the many scenes of human history moving in different directions and yet having in their own way a peculiar harmony and beauty? Or the same question may be put as an analogy to society: In what sense are all of society's multifaceted directions and impulses unified in a curious sort of symphony where all themes are hummed together though in different ways, and yet they make a good vibration?

Pushing

There are times when a person will experience outrage or anger toward other persons in the group. To be angry with another person is to respond to that person's standing in your way or frustrating some value that you feel is important. Rather than listen to angry feelings being channeled through words, some leaders of group processes have shown that it is more effective and a quicker route to understanding to let the anger be expressed in terms of certain structured physical relationships. One of these is called the hand press or hand push, in which two persons who are angry with each other stand face-to-face, with hands locked together and push. They are asked to push hard to feel the whole force of the other person's body. Their instructions are: "See if you can push the other person back, or see if you can protect yourself from being pushed around by the other person." Similar transactions can occur through Indian hand wrestling or pillow fighting. Note: These encounters may involve heavy exertion and should not be attempted by persons for whom such exertion is not desirable.

Comment: In our spiritual formation it may be crucial for us to learn to affirm ourselves in such a way that we do not compliantly let other persons push us around. Standing one's own ground may be an important moment of self-affirmation, although, of course, it can also be self-assertive and inauthentic. It is hardly healthy to store a fund of anger that remains totally unexpressed. We in the Western religious tradition have learned to suppress anger in ways that are often unhealthy, and therefore discovering a way to get anger out into the open may be an important part of our learning process. When someone is doing something that you experience as a limitation on you, or a frustration of your value system, then understandably you feel angry. Such anger should be communicated in a way that is socially benign.

Beholding

There will be times when the group members are not really in touch with each other and do not want to be. Each person hides within his own shell. When the predominant feeling is withdrawal, the leader might try an experience of sustained beholding. Everyone is asked to stand up and wander around the room. In the milling process the participants risk beholding other human beings and being beheld by them. "Risk the moments of eye-to-eye contact in which you allow yourself to come into the visual presence of your neighbor, and in which you allow yourself to be presented to him visually. Without speaking, simply behold your neighbor's being. Allow his body and his body movement to address you visually." After this has gone on for some time, the participants are asked to think back to one person in whose visual presence each felt especially affirmed. "Identify one beholding relationship in which there was a sense of comfort and ease. Go to that person (if someone else has chosen that person, then allow yourself to be chosen by someone else), and discuss the following: What was going on between us that enabled us to be at ease? How does it feel to really welcome another person into one's visual presence?"

If it is desirable to move a step farther into the spirit-formation question, ask: "What does it mean to be a body, and to say that my body is the gift of God? How do I at this moment experience my visual capacity as the valued gift of the Creator? How do I experience you and your selfhood as a valuable gift to me, as someone with whom I can risk simply being beheld and still be at ease?"

Another variation of this exercise is to ask: "Is there some person in whose presence you did not feel at ease, or who had difficulty beholding you? Go to that person and talk about why you felt uncomfortable in allowing yourself to come into the visual range of that person in any significant way."

In this case the spirit-formation question can be opened in a slightly different way by asking how our anxieties about being beheld reflect our anxieties about being a body. How can we better own up to having a body—the very body that we have—than by allowing that body to come into others' visual range? Does this have something to do with faith in God, or trust in the unfolding of being? How does the failure to behold others or the anxiety about being beheld by others point to a fundamental estrangement from others which in a sense is an indication of our deeper estrangement from life itself and the giver of life? How can we learn to own up better to those parts of our bodies which are not especially attractive and yet belong to us? If you do not like your body, what is your responsibility toward changing it where it can be changed?

Mirroring

Sometimes the capacity for cooperative action and empathy needs to be exercised and nurtured. A simple process through which this capacity can be cultivated in an elementary way is a mirroring exercise in which a group is divided into pairs, each pair standing face-to-face. Partners hold their hands up very close to each other, palms facing but not touching. When either person begins to move, the other partner moves with the one who is taking the initiative. Palms remain close, without touching. This is an exercise in learning to cooperate with another person's initiative, in allowing another to take initiative, or in taking initiative oneself. Note what happens when the initiative changes from one person to the other.

Comment: Learning to give up control may be important for some. Learning to take initiative may be important for others. Relinquishing control can be understood as a theological issue similar to the question of faith, or trusting in a process that is ultimately beyond one's control. Taking initiative also has its theological dimension in the question of exercising the freedom and power that is a part of the gift of being human.

Let us anticipate criticism at this point. Some will experience a feeling of sheer phoniness in doing something in order to create community. Describing exercises of this sort sometimes seems to presuppose that authentic intimacy and trust can be designed and fabricated through a series of programmed exercises. I want to take that criticism seriously, since in fact it has been the case that group processes have too often made this sort of naïve assumption. None of these experiences should be imposed on a group from outside its current awareness continuum. Rather, in all the cases I have suggested, each one of the experiences may be a fitting response to a particular need. In each case I have attempted to indicate the contexts to which these exercises may be an appropriate response, but one can only leave it to the perspicacity of the group or leader to determine when that context appears.

Persons who have worked a great deal with groups will recognize many of these processes. They have been borrowed and reshaped from a wide variety of sources.[2] They are included here and in these particular forms because they can be commended for potential use in Christian education, experimentation in worship, and the nurture of Christian community. The only way to respond to the charge of phoniness is to be aware each time we introduce an experience that it be introduced in a context to which it is indeed relevant and therefore exists as an authentic response instead of simply an imposed one.

Trust Circle

There are times when a group will be searching more explicitly for a higher level of trust. How far is it possible for us to entrust ourselves to others? That is a question people frequently ask in intensive groups. Often the behavior that will indicate these concerns will be body movements that express anxiety, withdrawal, and immobilization. Under these circumstances one nonverbal experience that is most useful in allowing people to test their trust level is the trust circle. Six to ten people stand in a small, fairly tight circle. One person stands in the middle. He is asked to close his eyes, plant his feet firmly in one spot, and hold his legs relatively stiff, but let the rest of his body relax. (The group is asked to remain silent.) He is to lean back and allow his body to fall into the hands of others. He will be passed around from hand to hand by the group and will experience, in a sequence of movements from one person's hands to another's, the support of the group. Often the group will

want to cradle the individual like a child, or sometimes
members will pick up his feet and rock him and in some
cases lift him above their heads and do whatever seems
appropriate to express nonverbally their care and concern for him. When they feel they have expressed what
they want to say to him, he is let down very gently on
the floor and allowed to lie there for as long as he wants
until he is ready to open his eyes. Then another person
can voluntarily move into the circle and do the same
thing until everyone has experienced the trust circle.

Comment: This experience can be extremely meaningful for several reasons. Persons who feel deprived in
terms of sensory comfort, persons who need to be cared
for or need to feel the affirmation of the group, persons
who have felt exclusion from the group, persons who are
hungry for the touch of others, persons who have been
constricted and anxious, may find it extremely gratifying
to be cared for in the arms of other persons and to feel
their support. The trust circle, devised by behavioral
scientists trying to facilitate group communication, has
important implications for Christian worship and Christian education. The Christian community is trying to
learn what it means to trust in God. The experiencing of
trust in a trusting human environment can be an important building block upon which one can nurture the experiencing of trust in the trustworthiness of God. More
will be said later about that analogy, but I think that
at this point we can at least say that here is a group
experience which helps persons to think concretely about
what it means to be trustworthy and what it means to
entrust oneself to another. The Biblical witness calls the
faithful man to exercise his level of trust, to practice the
life of trusting his movement toward the unknown, and

of sharing in a community of trust.

What are the limitations of this exercise? First of all, there are some physical limitations. Women wearing skirts may find it difficult to do this exercise. Slacks and comfortable clothing are recommended in all cases. If the persons doing the caring do not come across as truly caring persons, this manifests itself and it may become counter-productive. Furthermore, it should be understood that learning to trust in one's brothers is not the same as learning to trust in God, although it may be an edifying analogy.

Monitored Blind Walk

Many of the exercises we have talked about have been for small groups of six to twelve people. A much larger group of people may want to make some attempt to achieve a higher trust level in a short period of time. Under these conditions, the leader divides the group into two parts. One part constitutes a large outside ring, the other stands within the circle as individuals. The persons in the inside will walk with their eyes closed, first very cautiously, then at whatever pace they choose. They will expect the monitors of the outer circle to change their direction so they will not bump others or get into any trouble. Those on the outside should be aware that those on the inside are depending on them to keep them from getting hurt. After the inside group has walked for a while, the order is reversed, the outside people go inside, and the inside people go to the outside. A subsequent discussion, in pairs, focuses on the issues of risk, trust, and mutual accountability.

Feedback Cards

There are times in a group when the flow of energy is clogged up. Critical feedback is thwarted. Persons find it hard to give clear negative or positive feedback. Sometimes persons cannot get into the group. High participators are talking so much that the others cannot get their words in edgewise. This often happens in larger groups when a few persons may claim most of the air time and leave others out. One way to overcome this clogging is by the use of a simple procedure involving cards of two different colors, usually blue and red. Colored construction paper may be cut up into blue and red cards about two inches square. Set the cards out in the middle of the group, where everyone can have equal access to them. The instruction is simple: "If you feel positively toward something that someone has said or if you feel sympathetic toward it or moved by it or have a sense that you want to respond positively to it, then give that person a blue card. On the other hand, if you have a negative reaction or if you are angry about what someone is saying or if you don't like the way he is coming on or if he is doing something destructive to you or giving you bad feelings, then give him a red card." The group will experience a more rapid flow of interaction and many communications will be sent in a short time. The only other instruction is that if anyone wants to know why a color card was given to him, he has a right to ask the person who gave it.

What does this color card feedback procedure have to do with religious growth or spiritual formation? Giving and receiving feedback may be exceptionally difficult in modern society because many of us have been carefully trained to hide our feelings and simulate expressions. The principle to which the encounter culture would have us return again and again is the Ninth Commandment: "You shall not bear false witness against your neighbor." In daily interpersonal transactions, we often bear false witness indirectly by not sharing our actual responses to what others are saying and doing to us.

Color card feedback is an attempt to help persons not to bear false witness and to facilitate true witness to each other. It stimulates more accurate and readily available witness about what is happening between persons. Much of the encounter culture's ethic can be summarized under the single command not to bear false witness. For if persons are thoroughly honest with themselves and others, an encounter is taking place, regardless of where or under what conditions it occurs.

Luther was fond of saying that "a lie is like a snowball: the longer you roll it, the larger it becomes, and the stronger the sun shines the sooner it melts." [3] Elsewhere Luther spoke of a lie as "a fertile thing. One lie gives birth to seven other lies that are needed to give support to the first lie. Yet it is impossible for conscience to avoid rashly betraying itself—if not by words, then at least by its demeanor." [4] So it is that much effort in modern society is expended in trying to cover up for the lies we tell each other. Our body language or demeanor betrays that lying. It is against this ingrained societal dishonesty that the encounter culture is struggling.

2. BODY SPACE AND CONTROL

The Lift

Is it possible for one person radically to entrust the control of his muscles to the hands of another? This question may be addressed nonverbally in the following experience. The context: Often persons in a group are found to be deeply concerned about the control issue [5] (i.e., who controls whom; who is in charge of the group; who is influential; who is going to shape my life; how can I keep my own identity apart from you). When these kinds of questions are in the air, it is doubtful whether they can be worked out verbally.

One way to deal with them is to play "Lift." The leader invites participants to choose partners in this specific way: "Choose some person from whom you are at a distance, or with whom you feel some discomfort. Pairs should get into a place where they have free working space, preferably on a carpeted floor. One of the partners lies down comfortably on his back, and, eyes closed, tries to become fully relaxed, using deep breathing and letting the muscles fall limp. The other person is to cradle his partner's right wrist and lift it up very slowly and gently. See how slowly you can lift the hand and see how gently it can be cared for. Holding the wrist, let the hands and fingers fall completely limp. The point is to 'give away' muscular control. Do not move beyond the hand until you have experienced it in a relaxed and noncontrolling state. Then lift the entire right arm with the same concern. After the right arm is laid down very

gently, go to the left side and do the same. Allow plenty
of time for muscles to relax and limbs to be entrusted
to your control. Cradle the ankle so the leg is suspended
between the hip and the partner's hand. When the leg is
fully relaxed, let it descend gently to a resting position
and do the same thing with the other leg. Then put your
hands under your partner's head very gently and raise
his head off the floor. See if you can help your partner
to 'give his head away,' in a sense, into your hands. Communicate your concern, care, and trust tactilely. His head
is heavy. Hold it carefully. Let it down very gently. Then
change places with your partner and let him do the
same thing with you. When this is done, talk to each
other about what has happened to you both. Ask where
you have been enabled to trust each other in fresh ways
and where you have felt constricted."

Comment: This experience is all about relinquishing
control and being worthy of another's trust. "Letting go,"
or relinquishing control, has great significance in spiritual formation. The essence of the life of the spirit is
captured in Jesus' phrase, "Nevertheless not my will, but
thine, be done." Exercising the capacity to trust others
may be a step toward trusting the source and end of life.

The Hive

There are times when a group seems trapped, static,
immobile, unable to express animal feelings. Persons are
afraid of the depths of their own passions. At times like
this, the leader may invite the group to stand in a circle
and do the hive. Six to twelve persons kneel in a circle,
arm in arm, tightly clustered, with heads close together.
Begin the hive with a very low hum. The only instruc-

tions to the group are: "Take it slow and feel it as you go. Begin the hum very quietly and do not increase the pitch for quite a long time. Gradually begin to raise the level of the hum. Very slowly raise your bodies as the pitch rises. Build it very slowly, but as you come up, develop more volume until by the time you are at the top with hands outstretched high over your heads, everyone is letting out as much noise from his lungs as possible, with as much exuberance as possible. Let it all out. Let the animal feelings or oneness with the group or joy or rage or whatever else is happening come to their highest volume and pitch possible through the lungs and larynx and throat."

Afterward the group may sit down and ask the question, What is happening to us? What do we feel? What does it mean to share in a "tribal shout"? Is it possible to live comfortably with the animal and primitive part of man? What does it have to do with the Christian understanding of man? Man, who is capable of self-transcendence, imagination, and reason, does not cease to have animal passions that call out to be affirmed, sometimes at the tops of voices.

Body Space

There are times in the lives of some groups when there may be a desire to achieve closeness and yet a hesitancy on the part of individuals to move toward others. There may be times when individuals will be willing to withdraw into their own body space and live, as it were, a cocoon existence. In fact, that is the way many of us live most of our lives, only touching another person's body space in ritualized ways, such as shaking hands, or, if we get any closer, we may have all sorts of bizarre associations with sexual intimacy that make it difficult for us to be physically close to others.

If there is a hunger for closeness in the group but an inability to achieve it, there is a simple process that may help the group to move in that direction. This experience is often used as an "opener" for microlabs. The group sits on the floor in a circle, with eyes closed. The participants are far enough apart that no one is touching another and each has an identifiable space of his own. The leader says: "You might want to begin by doing some deep breathing, or simply listening to sounds, or attempting to get in touch with your own body processes: your heartbeat, your breathing, your musculature, the ebb and flow of your own body energies. Reach up and feel some of your space. Experience that space. Imagine that your space is immensely valuable, as if you had just discovered something of very great importance. Let your hands move through that space as if it were something greatly valued. Embrace the space; see if you can in effect hold it close to you as something precious; let your hands do what they want to do in the presence of that space. Touch the rug. Tap the floor that supports you. Feel its temperature, texture, resilience.

"The next step is to get in touch with your own body space. Experience by touch the size of your head and shoulders and arms and legs and torso and see if you can get a feel for the space that your body is displacing. Consider the place where you are sitting as your own territory. Now, eyes closed, allow your hands to reach out for others, and if you happen to touch another hand, experience what is there. Feel the flow of energy from that hand—its shape and solidity and pliability. Allow your body space to penetrate another person's body space and see what that does. See what you discover about yourself in a nonverbal, nonvisual meeting with another hand. What can you learn about that person's strength or compliance, his willingness to move toward you, or his unwillingness to do so? Open your eyes and talk with the person with whom you have shared space. What have you learned about yourself or about your partner?"

Now we will comment theologically on both phases of this experience—both the affirmation of one's own body space and interpenetration with others: In experiencing the preciousness of space, we can think with the Judeo-Christian tradition about the elemental gift of time and space as God's gift. The gift of creation involves the space to be. The kind of creation that God chooses is not a creation in which there is no space to be or no time to be. To take that elementary fact seriously is an awesome awareness. We need time in order to have space. Space without time would be immobile. Time without space would be homeless. Out of this experience a group may do some broad-ranging theological reflection on the question of what it means to experience oneself and others spatially.

The hand carries out the intent of the will. Much can be experienced of another person's energy and intention through the touch of his hand. Reaching out for others is analogous to God's reaching out for humanity. Fundamental to this exercise is the awareness that body space is shared. All existence is shared existence; or, to use Biblical language, covenant existence. Man's being is a being-with-others.

It is not accidental that the most powerful symbol of

the interpenetration of interpersonal space is sexuality, where two bodies, in effect, come together as one. The Biblical witness speaks of a *henosis,* where two persons become one flesh. Through risk and trust, two persons share fully their body space. Other less ecstatic or erotic forms of interpersonal closeness can also remind us of our covenant existence. A firm hand on a shoulder, a responsive embrace, even a warm handshake, can send a powerful message telling us again that we are not intended to live our lives alone. Discovering another person's body space may bring one into an awareness of interpersonal covenant that is deeply illuminated by the Biblical witness.

3. LIFE CYCLE FANTASY

There will be times when persons in a group will experience the need to embrace their lives as a totality and to recapitulate the whole of their experience in an imaginative act. These are the times when people ask elemental questions such as: What is the meaning of my life? Where have I come from? Where am I going? When persons wish to see their lives in a sort of synoptic focus or in a wholistic way, the group leader might invite the group to take the following fantasy trip:

Have each person in the group begin by selecting a spot that has sufficient living space in which to stretch out. It would be advisable for the group leader to have on hand an orchestral recording with both tranquil and tempestuous music. Begin by having all the participants lie down, close their eyes, and listen to the tranquil music addressing them.

As the music builds, the leader's instructions are: "You are in a cocoon. See whether you can experience this moment as if you were living in a cocoon. Feel the walls that surround you. Eyes closed, put your hands on the walls of your environment. See whether you like the environment you are in. If you prefer to be an inert, immobile, embryonic mass, then do what you feel like doing in the cocoon. It is warm and peaceful. It is a generous place to be. All your needs are supplied. Everything is protected. You are living in a safe place. Let yourself experience the security, the protection, that is your environment. (*Pause.*)

"Now you are beginning to hear the distant call of a different kind of life. You are experiencing the stirrings of birth. Something in you wishes to be born, to move out into a different world. You are beginning to realize that the cocoon is not what you were made for, but is only preliminary, or preparatory to what you shall be. You realize that it is possible to leave the cocoon and go into an unknown environment. If you would like to break out of the cocoon and go and explore the other environment, do that. Let your body do what you feel like doing. If you would like to remain inert, then you have to deal with the fact that the cocoon environment wishes to push you out and expel you. Let your body respond to the fact that you are being deprived of the safe cocoon environment. Now it is becoming clear that even if you wanted to stay in the cocoon, it would be impossible. You find yourself, eyes remaining closed, moving into a new and unknown environment. (*Pause.*)

"You are now in that new and unknown environment. Move your fingers and hands through the space of that world. Experience the new spatial environment into which you have come. Let your arms grasp as much of that space and penetrate as much of that space as you wish to. See whether your body works. As if for the first time, using your stomach and shoulder muscles, see how it feels to sit up. How does it feel to be in control of your own body instead of being in a constricted place? How does the freedom of spatial movement feel? See whether your feet and legs work in a way that will enable you to stand up and experience more of the open spatial environment that seems to be out there. (*Pause.*)

"Now, see whether it might be possible (as if for the first time) to move into that environment. Take a step. See whether your body will support you. Proceed very carefully as if you were not certain that you could move successfully but were trying it out. See whether it is possible to maintain your balance, so that when you take a step you do not fall down. Once you discover that it is possible to move, then move—very slowly at first—cautiously experiencing the space around you. Increasingly allow yourself to enjoy that space. It is a free space, free for your movement. You are no longer in the enclosed environment lacking possibilities out of which you came. Move around and let your hands touch whatever they happen to touch in your environment as though you were discovering it for the first time. Now, if by any chance you happen to meet some other being like yourself or an object of some kind, with eyes still closed allow yourself to discover what it is. Allow yourself to be discovered by other persons and in turn, attempt to discover them tactilely. Ask yourself how it feels to realize that you are not alone but sharing the space of this new world with others. Curiously you wonder about these beings in your presence. Touch their shoulders and arms and face and see whether you can learn something about them. See whether you think they are friendly or hostile. See whether you think they are like yourself or different from you. Can you trust these people, or must you protect yourself from them? (*Pause. Change from tranquil to tempestuous music.*)

"Now it appears that there is something threatening in the distance. You hear thunder. You are beginning to be aware that the universe in which you live has unknown elements which are frightening. There is an angry storm brewing in the distance and you feel it moving closer. As it comes nearer, you experience the need to draw nearer to those with whom you share this space. As the threatening sounds of the environment come closer, you begin to huddle closer together with the other beings in your environment. The storm is growing in intensity. It is very good to be close to others. You feel their warmth and you feel that you are in a safe place in the midst of a storm in which you might not survive alone. You are huddled tightly together, feeling the strength of your companions. If you have not found a group yet, search for one in which you can feel support and warmth in a time of extreme danger. (*Pause. If a participant is separated from a group, guide him toward one. Change to tranquil music.*)

"Now the storm is beginning to subside. Threats are still present, but you can feel them diminishing. A sigh of relief is felt among your companions. You begin to breathe more deeply. You feel more at home in your world. Let yourself say to your neighbors nonverbally, with your eyes closed, how it feels to have survived this threat with them, and how it feels to be with them in the midst of threat, how grateful you are to them for their presence, and how much they have meant to you. (*Pause.*)

"Now the world is getting brighter and the sun is beginning to break through the distant clouds. It is midday and you want to feel the warmth of the sun after the storm. Breathe deeply and let your hands stretch out and embrace the sun. Drink in as much of the sun as possible. Let it warm your being. Go and find some living space of your own and allow yourself to enjoy being yourself in the midst of the sun. You are in a safe place. There are no threats. You are in the midst of a friendly environment. It is good to be warmed by that environment. Let your spirit dance and bask in the sun. Let your body do what it wants to do in response to the beauty and joy and warmth of this day. Give your spirit time to taste the ecstasy of being in free space. You are glad that you have been born and have met others and have shared in being. (*Pause.*)

"Now you begin to realize faintly that it is time to go and that soon you must be saying good-by to your friends. You know that you cannot be in this free space forever and that it is time to go. The time has come for you to say good-by to your friends. Greet them in whatever way seems appropriate. Tell them what they have meant to you, and that it is now time for you to go. Nonverbally express your feelings toward other beings in your presence. (*Pause.*)

"When you feel that you have said to them all that you can say, all that you want to say about your being there with them, break off whatever relationship you have with them, and find a place to be alone. Find a place that seems right for you to be alone with yourself. When you have found that place, let it be a place where there is space for you to reflect on what you have been, what has happened to you, what sort of life you have experienced. Then let your body succumb to the pull of gravity. Let it relax. Let it lie down. Let gravity pull the weight of your body down to the earth, and allow yourself to give up the life that you have just completed. Allow yourself to affirm what has happened to you, to receive it as good, and to let it go. (*Pause.*)

"This is the time for letting go. It is the time for saying good-by to this life, to this experience. As you lie down comfortably, let the experience fade into nothingness. Allow yourself to be deprived of it, and accept the fact that you will not be there interminably. Give yourself time to give up the experiences you have had. Behold them, remember them, affirm them, receive them, and then give them up again. Let them go into nothingness. Let them be stored in the mind of God. (*Long pause.*)

"After you have fully experienced the process of giving up, and when you are ready, open your eyes and look around you. Sit up, and ask yourself: Who am I? Where have I been? What have I experienced? What does my life mean?" (*Participants may join with partners and talk about what happened to them, or, in groups of six to eight, discuss how they experienced the entire life-death cycle.*)

Comment: What does this experience say about birth and life and death that may be significant as an exercise in spiritual formation? Being born is a mythopoetic image which can apply not only to physical birth but to entering into any new environment. The whole of life is composed of a sequence of such entries. Constantly we are being asked to move into new environments. We are asked to be born into new relationships. We are asked to be born into new times and places, new social environments, new technological environments, new moral environments. This is what history is composed of: the constant process of being born and of dying in different ways, of receiving finite relationships and of giving them up.[6]

This experience is also a testing or re-experiencing of the ability to receive life spatially, to move into a spatial environment and to feel that space as a gift, or, in the language of the Christian community, to feel creation as a gift. The capacity of bodily movement is a great gift, and this exercise is a way of imaginatively reappropriating that gift. Again, movement is a symbolic way of expressing any sort of freedom, not just the movement that an infant experiences when he learns how to walk, but learning to receive joyfully any new spatial environment as a gift. When a child learns to take a step, he is learning about risk and trust. It is impossible to learn to walk unless one learns to trust one's own body mechanism, musculature, and the capacity of one's body to move through space and time. Such trusting is, in a certain sense, what Judeo-Christian faith is all about. The Biblical image of trusting in God, and of taking the first step in a new environment, has its prototype in Abraham's moving from the comfortable and known land of Ur into the unknown land of Canaan.

Not only is life lived together with others and loneliness overcome by others, but genuine support amid the threat of history and nature is possible through the sharing of one's life with others. This fantasy offers the possibility of imaginatively recapitulating the threat of nature and of feeling its power, while feeling the comfort of others in the face of that threat.

Finally, the fantasy gives us a context in which to think experientially in a new way about death. It brings us the opportunity to experience our death in an imaginative way, to own death, to receive death, to give up what we have been. Can I "be, through having been"? Can I face not being? Can I put it together? Can I bring it into some kind of integral focus? Can I accept what I have been? Do I despair over what I have been? Can I embrace my past being even with the awareness that there is no future? This fantasy provides a way of playing that out imaginatively. When it is clear that there is no more time, one must say good-by, express whatever gratitude one might feel toward one's friends, and let it go, let gravity pull one down to the earth and let one's own will simply recede into nothingness. That can be a profound growth experience. In Biblical language, the God who gives us life calls us also into death. Job says: "The LORD gave and the LORD has taken away; blessed be the name of the LORD." To learn to trust that reality which gives us life and to trust that same reality as the one to whom we return in death, is a powerful religious affirmation that may profoundly change the way one lives one's life. So as a whole this fantasy has theological components and implications for the religious awareness. It is possible to put it to work convincingly as a basis for exercising the imaginative spirit in its quest for human growth and integration.[7]

Chapter Two

THE NEW PIETISM

1. THE TRADITION AGAINST TRADITION

Carl Rogers views the basic encounter group as "the most rapidly spreading *social* invention of the century." [1] Although it is admittedly spreading rapidly, we doubt that it is an invention of this century. For although it indeed has returned in a powerful new focus in our time, its basic shape is a recurring pattern in the history of religious communities. We can see similar small-group encounter flourishing in the seventeenth and eighteenth centuries, especially among the radical, dissenting groups of Jewish and Protestant pietism.

The current encounter group is a demythologized and secularized form of a style of interpersonal encounter and community that is familiar to the history of religious communities in the West. The basic prototype of the encounter pattern is found in Protestant and Jewish pietism, which emphasized "here and now" experiencing, intensive small-group encounter, high trust levels in group interaction, honest confession amid a caring community, experimental mysticism, mutual pastoral care, extended conversion marathons, radical accountability to the group, an eclectic amalgam of resources for spiritual formation, intimate personal testimony, gut-level self-disclosure, brutally candid feedback procedures, anti-establishment social attitudes, and the laicization of leadership.[2] All these are the staples of the intensive group experience today. My purpose will be to demonstrate that there are direct analogies, too numerous to be accidental (and, I would also hypothesize,[3] a definable stream of historical influence), between small-group encounter in Protestant and Jewish religious movements, and the current encounter culture.

One of the things that has fascinated me about intensive group experiencing in its popular form today is its determined antihistorical bent. So single-minded is its focus upon the here and now that it tends to neglect any sort of dialogue with man's past. So determined is it to create a new future that it imagines that it has no past. It in fact continually lives out of the illusion that intensive group experiencing is something that belongs only to the last half of the twentieth century and never to any previous period. Of course this is just historical ignorance. But it says a great deal about the very history out of which it has come, namely, the history of individualistic, pragmatic romanticism, which is paradoxically a tradition against tradition.

Facilitators who work with group processes are not accustomed to thinking historically, yet their work inevitably exists in a historical continuum that deserves to be made much clearer. So busy have the encounter culture gurus been in turning people on to "the now" that it has not occurred to them that anyone else ever could have done this before them. Not uncommonly we find among them a flippant polemic even against the raising of historical consciousness. One might suspect that some fear being discovered as "old hat." The most damning description that can be addressed to any encounter group or encounter group leader is that they are doing something old-fashioned. There is an insatiable hunger in the movement for novelty. There is a corresponding embarrassment and disgust with history. There is a common assumption that man's future is all that is worthwhile, his past merely an obstacle to be transcended. Thus it is not surprising that there is a dire neglect of study and lack of awareness of the antecedents and historic prototypes of the encounter movement.

Henry Ford's unforgettable maxim "History is bunk" captures a characteristically American pragmatic attitude that is deeply engrained in the group processes movement. There is not only a general dearth of historical awareness (a kinder term than historical ignorance) but also smug self-satisfaction among groups that "we" have discovered something fabulously "new" (the real magic word of the twentieth century). It is a curious form of modern *hubris,* which surely someday will be viewed as myopia. With astonishing self-assurance, the movement assumes that the only significant moment of history is the present, that the last single decade is of more value than the remainder of the past century, and that the past century is of infinitely more value to knowledge than all previous centuries combined.

Accordingly, the limited attempts to account historically for the encounter group movement and group psychotherapy make no attempt to reach back more than a hundred years, and most of them go back only fifty years or less.[4] Various accounts date the beginnings of the group processes movement with Jacob Moreno in 1910,

Joseph Pratt in 1905, Cody Marsh in 1930, or Kenneth Benne in the early 1940's.[5] Standard texts in group dynamics attribute the earliest innovations to Kurt Lewin in the 1930's, Muzafer Sherif in 1936, W. R. Bion in the 1940's. Some interpreters venture to go as far back as Durkheim, Simmel, Comte, Spencer, Cooley, Mead, Ward, Freud, McDougall, F. H. Allport, and others. None of these sources, however, addresses the eighteenth-century religious societies where the basic prototypes of the current encounter group are clearly to be found on a vast scale in a highly refined form as a vigorous and popular lay movement.

To say that the encounter culture is unconscious of its sources does not mean that it must be exhaustively conscious of those sources in order to function effectively at the operational level. But we would suppose that some heightened awareness of its historic origins would help it to avoid some of its messianic illusions or romantic conceptions of its own novelty. A part of what makes the group processes movement a "movement," however, is its curious conception of itself as something entirely new and uniquely promising for the future of mankind. Without this persistent historical narcissism, it could not have developed the strong "movement" character that it now has.

The encounter impresarios have extended the helpful therapeutic dictum of "staying in the here and now" into a general maxim of historical awareness. The only history they know is the history they are pretending to make. Yet, sadly enough, they remain blind to the very historical forces that enable them to think the way they think and to frame the issues the way they frame them. One never hears mentioned among them the names of

Renaissance men such as Pico della Mirandola or Leon Battista Alberti, who, like them, were supremely confident of the capacity of man for self-transformation, and who inaugurated another vast "human potential movement," which we call the Renaissance. They know or speak little of the "heavenly vision of the eighteenth century philosophers" of which Carl Becker has so delightfully written, which in so many ways shapes the philosophical underpinnings of their romanticisms.[6] They have not studied the utopias of the sixteenth or nineteenth centuries, which in decisive ways predate their own utopian hopes.

So there remains a vast historical labor that needs to be done in order to bring the movement into clearer self-awareness. But my focus here will be on one principal pattern from which the encounter culture today has most decisively borrowed as a model for social interaction and growth, viz., the encounter style of Protestant and Jewish pietism in the seventeenth, eighteenth, and nineteenth centuries.

2. THE DEMYTHOLOGIZING OF PIETISTIC ENCOUNTER

A highly mobile charismatic itinerancy was the prevalent model for ministry in frontier American pietism. Faced with a frontier in constant flux not unlike our "temporary society," these itinerant charismatic leaders moved constantly on horseback from small lay group to small lay group, facilitating their growth. Energized by visions of vast and rapid human change, armed with eclectic resources, and fascinated by experimental social interaction, they were accustomed to brutally honest feedback procedures.[7]

Similarly today the encounter change agents have combined a broad spectrum of resources with tough-minded feedback procedures to facilitate rapid growth in a mobile social context. The frontier model of itinerancy has been reappropriated as the prevalent model for leadership among the group facilitators today. From weekend to weekend they go on the "sawdust trail," converting, turning people on, building communities of growth and trust. They move from growth center to growth center, from happening to happening, from revival to revival, trying to re-energize the movement, teaching the latest techniques, ever faithful to the apostolic witnesses of the encounter culture (the canonical saints Perls, Maslow, Rogers, Reich, and Watts), encouraging pilgrimages to holy places like Bethel (!) and the healing waters of Esalen.

The social conditions to which the encounter culture is responding (mobility, depersonalization, emotive paralysis, the breakdown of authoritarian traditions) are almost identical to the conditions against which Protestant and Jewish pietism were protesting.[8] Rogers correctly observes that the small-group movement "has grown up entirely outside the 'establishment.' Most universities still look upon it with scorn. . . . The established professions of clinical psychology and psychiatry have stayed aloof, while the political right wing is certain that it represents a deep-seated Communist plot." Each of these features has its parallel in the anti-establishment mentality of left wing experiential pietism, which was looked upon with deep suspicion in its day by the Lutheran, Anglican, and Jewish religious establishments and by the universities. In some cases it was literally driven out of the land because of its seemingly radical character. It too was interpreted as an extremist plot against common order.

The Jewish form of pietism is Hasidism. Hasid refers to the righteous or the pious. The Hasidism that arose among remote Polish and Ukranian Jewish communities in the eighteenth century is remarkably similar to the spirit of Protestant pietism. It too was not primarily concerned with correct dogma or ritual but with the actual appropriation of the life of faith in community.

By the eighteenth century, Judaism was ready for a reaction against certain ascetic forms of rabbinical orthodoxy that emphasized fasting, penance, and "spiritual sadness." Hasidism was a response to the desire of ordinary people for a joyful, emotively satisfying faith applied practically in a social context. The aim of Hasidism was not to change belief but to change the believer. Concrete experiencing in the here and now was more important than abstract conceptualizing.[9]

A prominent feature of all forms of pietism, as well as of the current encounter culture, is the concept of a spiritual breakthrough of intense emotive depth that changes behavior radically. The literature of pietism is filled with testimonials of persons who have undergone sudden and radical conversion experiences.[10] Typically, after having first experienced themselves as being crushed by guilt and despair, they then describe how, within a supportive group, a radical turning point is experienced in which they feel deeply the acceptance and grace of God, whereupon a rich flow of gratitude and freedom motivates them to reshape their behavior. This is the center of the pietistic conversion experience, epitomized best by John Wesley's feeling his heart "strangely warmed" when an assurance was given him that Christ "had taken away my sins, even mine."

Compare this with an account written by a member of a basic encounter group (quoted by Rogers): "I had really buried under a layer of concrete many feelings I was afraid people were going to laugh at or stomp on, which, needless to say, was working all kinds of hell on my family and on me. . . . The real turning point for me was a simple gesture on your part of putting your arm around my shoulder one afternoon when I had made some crack about you not being a member of the group—that no one could cry on your shoulder. In my notes I had written the night before, 'There is no man in the world who loves me!' You seemed to be so genuinely concerned that day I was overwhelmed! . . . I *received* the gesture as one of the first feelings of acceptance—of me, just the dumb way I am, prickles and all—that I had ever experienced. I have felt needed, loving, competent, furious, frantic, anything and everything but just plain *loved*. You can imagine the flood of gratitude, humility, release that swept over me. I wrote with considerable joy, '*I* actually felt *loved*.' I doubt that I shall soon forget it." [11]

In probing these striking similarities, I am not arguing that modern group process leaders have been overtly or even secretly reading the literature of Protestant or Jewish pietism. The fact that they would not wish to be caught dead doing so, however, interests me immensely. A curious part of the task of historical inquiry is to show why they have preferred *not* to behold their own history, and why they have not analyzed the subtle and indirect forms in which they have unselfconsciously reappropriated and transmuted an available religious tradition. These pietistic patterns were quietly and inertly "in the air" as available social models for the progenitors of current group encounter such as Lewin, Moreno, Rogers, and the National Training Laboratories innovators.[12] The fact that they were borrowed and applied *unconsciously* rather than consciously is noteworthy, to say the least, especially among therapists so deliberately committed to "making the unconscious conscious."

I want to avoid the reductionist impression that current encounter group processes can be boiled down essentially to what was taking place in the eighteenth-century religious societies. I am trying, rather, to unveil the striking similarities between the two movements, and in a modest way to hypothesize that there may be some discernible flow of influence from the pietistic encounter style to the current encounter style.

Jewish and Protestant pietism have both been, like current encounter groups, highly syncretistic movements. Wesley's movement, for example, was a practical synthesis of Puritan and Anglican (or more broadly Protestant and Catholic) traditions of faith and practice and communal life. Few of the parts of the synthesis were original with him, but his putting them together in a practical focus, easily implemented in small groups, was a unique and gifted contribution.[13] Likewise, it is of the essence of the encounter culture today that it is syncretistic, putting a broad range of change strategies together into a working, practical synthesis of resources for human growth in small groups.

A system of approaches so eclectic can hardly be the work of a single man or narrow group of men. Nor can it be the product of a single generation. Rather, so complex and varied are these resources that it seems more plausible that they have emerged through a long series of cultural mutations and only through the achievement of several generations of intensive communities experimenting with personal growth.

It is regrettable that we are compelled to use the historian's term "pietism" to describe a movement so creative and variegated, since that term has been so badly abused by a long tradition of religious experience which often bordered on fanaticism and anti-intellectualism. Some historians distinguish between *classical pietism* of the seventeenth and eighteenth centuries and a later or *deteriorating pietism* of the late nineteenth and twentieth centuries when the original genius had long been spent.[14] It is regrettable that when the term "pietism" is currently used, it usually points not to that classical movement which spawned so many creative impulses in Western history but rather to that deteriorated form of introverted, self-concerned, self-righteous fanaticism in its most undesirable and caricatured forms. Although classical pietism is still the nomenclature preferred by historians who mark the developments from Spener, Zinzendorf, and the Baal Shem-Tob to the Blumhardts, Finney, and Mordecai of Lekhovitz, we might also correctly refer to this period as a movement of "experiential small group religious innovation." [15]

My intent is not to debunk encounter groups by showing their supposedly embarrassing historical origins. Doubtless some who are only willing to deal lightly with our hypothesis may draw that erroneous conclusion. Rather, I am attempting to be positively supportive of the encounter culture precisely through showing that its historic origins are unconsciously in touch with rich Western religious resources from which it now considers itself to be estranged. Though often despised and vilified, the classical pietistic tradition was far more innovative than its reputation for rigidity would indicate.[16] Both Jewish and Protestant pietism have been profoundly instrumental in liberating the Western tradition from the strictures of scholastic orthodoxy and in helping to introduce it to the modern world, focusing on the experiencing moral subject, which became the overriding theme of liberal theology from Kant and Schleiermacher to the present.

So our motivation is hardly to scandalize the encounter culture. Rather, we are hoping to discover the functional historical models that have enabled the encounter culture today to become as promising and creative as it is. We are pressing for a sympathetic yet critical restudy of both pietistic encounter and contemporary encounter in the hope that their unrecognized kinship might be deemed serendipitous by both parties.

The question remains as to why the otherwise intelligent proponents of the intensive group experience in the twentieth century have not mentioned or even recognized their Protestant and Jewish pietistic origins. If we reflect carefully, however, their reasons for not wishing to discuss this relationship have been, from a practical point of view, understandable. Quite simply, the tradition of emotive and quasi-fanatical pietism has long been out of favor with the socially mobile intelligentsia and cultural *avant-garde* who form the clientele of the encounter culture. In fact, the pietistic tradition is radically out of favor today with almost everyone, including not only the universities and the historians but also the seminaries, and even the churches and synagogues that pietism has spawned. Pietistic words such as "revival" and "religion of the heart" and "conversion" and "testimony" are repulsive to self-consciously modern men. The irony, of course, is that although the words are no longer acceptable, all the meanings that those words freighted have been taken right back into the heart of the encounter culture.

In a similar vein, David Bakan has shown that Freud had convincing practical reasons for not wishing to reveal his roots in Jewish mysticism, since anti-Semitism was rife in his Viennese context and "to indicate the Jewish sources of his ideas would have dangerously exposed an intrinsically controversial theory to an unnecessary and possibly fatal opposition." [17] Bakan plausibly demonstrates that "Freud would have had good reason to *deliberately conceal* his sources if he were conscious that psychoanalysis was a development in the tradition of Jewish mysticism." [18] Likewise we believe that the encounter leaders would have good reason deliberately and circumspectly to hope that their roots might remain hidden (even if inadvertently by failing to inquire into them), if they suspected that those roots might have made them look scandalous, fanatic, anti-intellectual, or, in a word, "pietistic" to their upwardly mobile liberal clientele.

We cannot ignore a curious form of dissimulation in the movement. If you can convince the encounter clientele that the meditation they are doing comes from Eastern religions, and not from the West, you can proceed amiably. If you can apply language like chakra, satori, and karma to your interpretations, instead of using their ordinary Western equivalents (which actually are more in touch with where the clientele is), you will find ready hearers, even though that language comes from authoritarian traditions which would be *ipso facto* rejected if they were Western. A group leader probably will be more acceptable if he can persuade his hearers that the "peak experiences" which he is programming have nothing to do with Western religion, and if Western, certainly not Protestant, and if Protestant, certainly not Calvinistic puritanism, and if Calvinism, certainly not pietism, against which they understand themselves to be most certainly rebelling.

Puritanism is doubtless the worst of words in the encounter vocabulary. The irony, of course, is that it is precisely the pietistic wing of the puritan Protestant tradition (so strongly influenced by English Calvinist dissent) which is being reappropriated in current encounter groups. Thus the deepest roots of the encounter movement are in the least likely of all places: in Calvinism more than in any other religious tradition, including all Hindu and Buddhist themes combined. In fact, the Zen and yoga themes which have been so overtly incorporated into the encounter culture have largely been absorbed into a world view decisively shaped by puritan Protestantism. In fact, the Americanized Zen and yoga often become unrecognizable to Easterners. So it is a curious self-deception to imagine that the deeper motivating forces behind the encounter culture come from Eastern religions. If and when the actual historical models are carefully clarified, this self-deception will be more and more difficult to sustain.[19]

3. COMPARISON OF THE PIETISTIC ENCOUNTER STYLES WITH CURRENT ENCOUNTER

The following quotations are placed in two columns in order to clarify similarities between small-group encounter styles of free-church Protestantism and those of the contemporary encounter culture. Although a much more detailed analysis could be made, these quotations provide a brief sampling of the similar approaches in five basic areas:

A. The Small-Group Format
B. The Zealous Pursuit of Honesty
C. Focus on Here and Now Experiencing
D. The Nurture of Intimacy
E. Revival as Marathon

Statements from eighteenth- and nineteenth-century pietistic writings in the left column may be compared with statements in the right column from the principal leaders of the encounter culture today—Perls, Rogers, Maslow, Schutz, and others.

[A] THE SMALL-GROUP FORMAT

EIGHTEENTH- AND NINETEENTH-CENTURY RELIGIOUS GROUP ENCOUNTER STYLES	CURRENT ENCOUNTER GROUP STYLES
Let each member of the class relate his experience with freedom and simplicity. The design of the classes is to ascertain the	All communication in the group should be as open and honest as it's possible to be. . . . Learn how to be more open with every-

spiritual state of each member, in order that religious sympathy be excited, mutual regard promoted, mutual encouragement obtained.—*Rosser, 1855.*[20]

They had no need of being incumbered with many rules; having the best rule of all in their hearts. *No peculiar directions* were therefore given to them. . . . Everyone here has an equal liberty of speaking, there being none greater or less than another. . . . I often found the advantage of such a free conversation, and that "in the multitude of counsellors there is safety."—*Wesley, 1748.*[22]

I desired a small number . . . to spend an hour with me every Monday morning. My design was, not only to . . . incite them to love one another more, and to watch more carefully over each other, but also to have a select company, to whom I might unbosom myself on all occasions, without reserve.—*Wesley, 1748.*[24]

They began to "bear one another's burdens," and naturally

one, including yourself. . . . Talk directly to the person addressed.—*Schutz, 1971.*[21]

This group will meet for many hours and will serve as a kind of laboratory where each individual can increase his understanding of the forces which influence individual behavior and the performance of groups and organizations. The data for learning will be our own behavior, feelings, and reactions. We begin with *no definite structure* or organization, no agreed-upon procedures, and no specific agenda. It will be up to us to fill the vacuum created by the lack of these familiar elements and to study our group as we evolve. . . . With these few comments, I think we are ready to begin in whatever way you feel will be most helpful.—*Seashore, 1968.*[23]

The deeper you go the safer it is. If you go deep the group gets close. People begin caring for each other and supporting each other.—*Schutz, quoted by Gustaitis, 1969.*[25]

A climate of mutual trust develops out of this mutual free-to "care for each other." As they had daily a more intimate acquaintance with, so they had a more endearing affection for, each other.—*Wesley, 1748.*[26]

dom to express real feelings, positive and negative.—*Rogers, 1970.*[27]

[B] THE ZEALOUS PURSUIT OF HONESTY

Do you desire that every one of us should tell you, from time to time, whatsoever is in his heart concerning you? Consider! Do you desire we should tell you whatsoever we think, whatsoever we fear, whatsoever we hear concerning you?—*Wesley, 1744.*[28]

Feedback is most acceptable when the receiver himself has formulated the question which those observing him can answer. It is *solicited,* rather than imposed.—*National Training Laboratories, 1968.*[29]

Do you desire to be told of your faults?—*Wesley, 1744.*[30]

Discover your resistances.— *Perls and others, 1951.*[31]

Rules of the Bands:
To speak each of us in order, freely and plainly, the true state of our souls, with the faults we have committed in thought, word, or deed, and the temptations we have felt since our last meeting.—*Wesley, 1744.*[32]

Self-examination, severe, thorough, impartial. The class meeting will be productive of but little real, lasting benefit without this.—*Rosser, 1855.*[33]

The assumption in your groups seems to be, on the contrary, that people are very tough, and not brittle. They can take an awful lot. The best thing to do is get right at them, and not to sneak up on them, or be delicate with them, or try to surround them from the rear. Get right smack into the middle of things right away. I've suggested that a name for this might be "no-crap therapy." It serves to clean out the defenses, the rationalizations, the veils, the evasions and politeness of the world.—*Maslow, 1967.*[34]

Rules of the Bands:
Is it your desire and design to be, on this and all other occa-

The pursuit of honesty is begun by asking the couples to think of three secrets they have never

sions, entirely open, so as to speak everything that is in your heart without exception, without disguise and without reserve? Have you nothing you desire to keep secret?—*Wesley, 1744.*[35]

What known sins have you committed since our last meeting?—*Wesley, 1744.*[37]

Rules of the Bands:
To desire some person among us to speak his own state first, and then to ask the rest, in order, as many and as searching questions as may be, concerning their state, sins and temptations.—*Wesley, 1744.*[39]

Falsehoods are many, but truth is one.—*Rabbi Nachman Bratzlaver, 1810.*[41]

told their mate and that would be most likely to jeopardize their relationship. During the course of the workshop they tell these secrets.—*Schutz, 1971.*[36]

I force my groups to be open, to tell me everything.—*Schutz, 1971.*[38]

Making the rounds. The therapist may feel that a particular theme or feeling expressed by the patient should be faced vis a vis every other person in the group. The patient may have said, "I can't stand anyone in this room." Therapist: "O.K., make the rounds. Say that to each one of us and add some other remark pertaining to your feelings about each person."—*Levitsky, 1969.*[40]

As open encounter proceeds and gets more profound, as intrapsychic methods get deeper. . . . I see man's unity and oneness more clearly.—*Schutz, 1971.*[42]

[C] FOCUS ON HERE AND NOW EXPERIENCING

Let your expressions be clear and definite, pointed and brief, having reference to your present experience, so that the state of your mind may be easily apprehended.—*Newstead, 1843.*[43]

Realize (make real) the nowness of your experience.—*Perls, 1969.*[44]

Beware of resting in past experience.—*Newstead, 1843.*[45]

Prayer in the class-room is special, and is concentrated upon some present object, and this explains, to some degree, its power.—*Rosser, 1855.*[47]

An ingenuous account of our temptations is the surest way to subdue them.—*Rosser, 1855.*[49]

Do you desire that, in doing this, we should come as close as possible; that we should cut to the quick, and search your heart to the bottom?—*Wesley, 1744.*[51]

Shun the very appearance of affectation. Let your words and your manner be perfectly natural. Do not . . . speak in borrowed nor hackneyed terms, lest it should become a merely formal exercise, and consequently a deceptive one.—*Newstead, 1843.*[53]

In the evening I went very unwillingly to a society in Aldersgate Street, where one was reading Luther's preface to the Epistle to the Romans. About a quarter before nine, while he was describing the

Nothing exists except the now. —*Perls, quoted by Gustaitis, 1969.*[46]
Stay with the here and now as much as possible.—*Schutz, 1971.*[48]

The principle is, "Can you stay with this feeling?" This technique is invoked at key moments when the patient refers to a feeling or mood or state of mind which is unpleasant and which he has a great urge to dispel. . . . The therapist says, "Can you stay with this feeling?"—*Levitsky, 1969.*[50]

I and thou; here and now.— *Perls, 1969.*[52]

Words are special culprits in the effort to avoid personal confrontation.—*Schutz, 1967.*[54]

Go to your core—focus, connect to yourself and then to the others with you, and surrender yourself fully to the feeling from your core.—*Lewis and Streitfeld, 1970.*[56]

change which God works in the heart through faith in Christ, I felt my heart strangely warmed. I felt I did trust in Christ, Christ alone, for salvation; and an assurance was given me, that He had taken away my sins, even mine, and saved me from the law of sin and death.—*Wesley, 1738.*[55]

[D] THE NURTURE OF INTIMACY

Many, many a time, in immediate answer to prayer, in the class-room, so intensely burns the heart with love to God and man, that the whole class is quickened by the subduing and stirring testimony given, and the very class-room seems to be a mansion of glory. —*Rosser, 1855.*[57]

Participants feel a closeness and intimacy which they have not felt even with their spouses or members of their own family, because they have revealed themselves here more deeply.— *Rogers, 1970.*[58]

When a happy correspondence between the outward walk and inward piety of believers is discovered, which can be known only by the disclosure of the interior life, we are not only prepared to comfort, encourage and strengthen one another, but form an intimacy of the holiest nature, a union of the strongest character.—*Rosser, 1855.*[59]

Where all is known and all accepted . . . further growth becomes possible. . . . To his astonishment, he finds that he is more accepted the more real that he becomes.—*Rogers, 1970.*[60]

If we yield to the suggestions that our distresses are the most deplorable, that our sins are so heinous that they ought not to be disclosed, or are so trivial that they need not be confessed, . . . or that we should give an unfair and partial account of

This willingness to take the risk of being one's inner self is certainly one of the steps toward relieving the loneliness that exists in each one of us and putting us in genuine touch with other human beings. A college student expressed this our true state, . . . and refer in but an obscure manner to whatever in us is disagreeable and unfavorable . . . our testimony in all these cases amounts to nothing more than a hurtful illusion.—*Rosser, 1855.*[61]

Tell your experience; and tell your conflicts; and tell your comforts. As iron sharpeneth iron, as rubbing of the hands maketh both warm, and as live coals maketh the rest to burn, so let the fruit of society be mutually sharpening, warming, and influencing.—*Rosser, 1855.*[63]

> We all partake the joy of one;
> The common peace we feel:
> A peace to sensual minds unknown,
> A joy unspeakable.
>
> And if our fellowship below
> In Jesus be so sweet,
> What height of rapture shall we know
> When round his throne we meet!
> —*Charles Wesley, hymn, 1749.*[65]

Brother, is thy heart with mine, as my heart is with thy heart? If it be, give me thy hand.— *Wesley, 1742.*[66]

risk very well when he said, "I felt at a loss today in that encounter group. Very naked. Now everyone knows too much about me; at the same time I am more comfortable in the knowledge that I don't have to put on my 'cool.'"—*Rogers, 1970.*[62]

To discover that a whole group of people finds it much easier to care for the real self than for the external facade is always a moving experience.— *Rogers, 1970.*[64]

One point at which open encounter and a mystical viewpoint are mutually helpful occurs when an encounter is going very deep. After hostility is worked through and differences acknowledged as people reach the deeper layers of personality, the similarity of all men becomes clearer. We are all in the same struggle but using different paths with different defenses. The notion that we are all one is given great meaning at these almost mystical moments in the group's life. —*Schutz, 1971.*[67]

[E] REVIVAL AS MARATHON [68]

In this revival originated our camp-meetings, and in both these denominations they were held every year, and, indeed, have been ever since, more or less. They would erect their camps with logs or frame them, and cover them with clapboards or shingles . . . and here they would collect together from forty to fifty miles around, sometimes further than that. Ten, twenty, and sometimes thirty ministers, of different denominations, would come together and preach night and day, four or five days together; and, indeed, I have known these camp-meetings to last three or four weeks, and great good resulted from them. . . . I have seen and heard more than five hundred Christians all shouting aloud the high praises of God at once.—*Cartwright, 1856.*[69]

The fountains of sin need to be broken up. In a true revival, Christians are always brought under such convictions; they see their sins in such a light, that often they find it impossible to maintain a hope of their acceptance. . . . The first step is a deep repentance, a breaking down of heart, a getting down into the dust before God, with deep humility, and forsaking sin—*Finney, 1834.*[72]

The marathon is not unlike a "pressure cooker" in which phony steam boils away and genuine emotions (including negative ones) emerge. The group atmosphere is kept focused every moment on the objectives at hand: to produce *change in orientation* and new ways of dealing with old crucial problems.—*Bach, 1966.*[70]

These experiences led me to the conclusion that the depth that could be reached in a concentrated workshop was so remarkable compared to the other approaches that I have virtually abandoned all other patterns. . . . I've found . . . that one intensive week is equivalent to two or three years of periodic therapy sessions, and that groups are much more effective than individual sessions.—*Schutz, 1971.*[71]

A chronically contracted muscle is in effect saying, "no." . . . Lying on a bed with a foam mattress he is asked to strike the bed repeatedly with his fists and say "no" with each blow in a loud and convincing tone. . . . At this point the group may encourage the subject to "let go," to pound with all his strength and yell with all his might.—*Ruitenbeek, 1970.*[73]

I have been at meetings where the whole congregation would be bathed in tears; and sometimes their cries would be so loud that the preacher's voice could not be heard. Some would be seized with trembling, and in a few moments drop on the floor as if they were dead; while others were embracing each other with streaming eyes, and all were lost in wonder, love and praise.—*Lee, 1810.*[74]

Participants almost unanimously speak of marathons, immediately afterward and a year afterward, as a worthwhile and moving experience. The words, "I felt reborn" are often uttered.—*Mintz, 1967.*[75]

With regard to these prudential helps we are continually changing one thing after another. [This] is not a weakness or fault, as you imagine, but a peculiar advantage which we enjoy. By this means we declare them all to be merely prudential, not essential, not of divine institution. We prevent, so far as in us lies, their growing formal or dead. We are always open to instruction; willing to be wiser every day than we were before. *Wesley, 1748.*[76]

The "open encounter group" . . . implies that the method is always changing and evolving. The groups we run today are run very differently from last year's and next year's groups. —*Schutz, 1971.*[77]

4. THE SOFT REVOLUTION: THEN AND NOW

I have found my curiosity unsquelchably aroused by the remarkable fact that the pietistic tradition and the current encounter culture had their birth in the same city, Frankfurt. As we compare the two movements, it is incredible how much of the initiating activity in both of them came from the same specific Rhineland locale. Let me be more specific. In the 1920's, Frankfurt was the unlikely place where a group of remarkably talented people came together, many of them Jews, many psychoanalytically oriented, many of whom eventually came to the United States. These innovators became the principal progenitors of the encounter group movement, group therapy, and the intensive group experience.[78] Even today they remain the "saints" of the movement. Frederick Perls, the chief exponent of Gestalt therapy, was in therapy in Frankfurt with Wilhelm Reich, who developed the concept of body armor so crucial to bioenergetics and Esalen. Martin Buber, the great Jewish philosopher so deeply drawn to hasidic Judaism, was in Frankfurt at the same time developing the philosophy of encounter, *I and Thou,* which had profound impact upon virtually all the existential psychotherapists, as well as upon Carl Rogers, the Gestalt therapists, and Jacob Moreno, who invented psychodrama. Paul Tillich was also in Frankfurt during this creative period. His discussions of *The Courage to Be* and *Theology of Culture* were later to stand as the most important Protestant theological contributions to the encounter culture. Kurt Goldstein, one of the most widely respected resources in the "third force" in psychology, or humanistic psychology, was also in this group, as were Helene Deutsch and Karen Horney. The small but distinguished faculty of the Institut für Sozialforschung at Goethe University in Frankfurt in the late 1920's and early 1930's included Herbert Marcuse, Erich Fromm, Franz Neumann, Theodor Adorno, Frederick Pollock, and Max Horkheimer.[79] Of more importance to the encounter culture, however, was Kurt Lewin, whose experiments with group processes and conflict have often been called the beginnings of the group dynamics movement. Lewin is one of the main theoretical resources for the National Training Laboratories development of T-groups.

That in itself is a remarkable collection of people, all influential in the history of the encounter culture, which surprisingly enough flowered not in Germany but in America. The more fascinating observation, however, is that just three hundred years ago a similar band of small-group innovators led by Philip Jacob Spener and August Hermann Francke, launched a movement which appears to be the basic prototype of the encounter culture in the same city of Frankfurt! Spener wrote *Pia desideria* in 1675 in Frankfurt, and there he gathered together a small group of persons dedicated to personal religious growth through intensive dialogue and mutual care for one another.[80]

If Vienna is the heartland for the genesis of psychoanalysis, surely Frankfurt, the city of Spener and the mother of Protestant pietism, must be accounted the seminal heartland of the encounter culture. Although it is more speculative as a historical thesis than I wish to put forth, I hope that someday scholars will inquire more deliberately into the curious coincidence that out of a single city two very similar types of encounter movements were spawned, with much the same methods and self-understanding, similar intentions, and against which identical objections have been raised, even though they stand three hundred years apart.

The words "pious" and "piety" have an exceptionally unsavory and unattractive sound to modern ears. Pious originally meant dutiful, or sensitive to the duties owed by creatures to God. Piety came later to refer to actions practiced for the sake of religious commitment, or under the appearance of religious commitment. Only in the modern period has the term taken on the nuance of hypocrisy and inauthenticity.

The term "pietas" was applied in derision to the followers of Spener in reference to the *collegia pietatis* or religious groups formed in Frankfurt around 1670. A pietist is one who lays stress upon a "religion of the heart," the depths of religious feeling, the relevance of faith for the totality of life, and the nurturing of faith in a small testimonial group.[81]

Spener was attempting to facilitate personal growth and religious faith through corporate accountability. The groups he brought together in his own home were searching for an intensification of the life of the spirit and a practical embodiment of the priesthood of all believers. Spener was less interested in controversy and polemic than in the development of the practice of love and forgiveness in small groups.[82]

Many features of Spener's earliest efforts at religious group encounter may be found in contemporary group processes virtually without change. Reacting against an elite, remote, self-satisfied professionalism, Spener affirmed the priesthood of all believers in an eminently practical way by developing small communities in which priestly functions were practiced by laity. He was oriented toward the practical implementation of behavioral change rather than its theoretical aspects. He exhibited a broad spirit of toleration and a primitive ecumenism that later became a central feature of pietistic faith and practice, as we note in Wesley's sermon on "The Catholic Spirit" and in Schleiermacher's ecclesiology.[83] Just as many encounter leaders today are interested in educational reform (Rogers, Schutz, and Leonard),[84] so were Spener, Francke, and their associ-

ates critics of their educational system, and for many of
the same reasons. They thought that education should
nurture wholistic personal growth, rather than confine
itself merely to cognitive learning.

Many of the criticisms made against pietism are often
heard today against the human potential movement—
fanaticism, anti-intellectualism, amateurish fascination
with mystical states, visions, trances, traumas and hal-
lucinatory states, and a lack of professionalism. Spener
was accused of enthusiasm and eccentricity, of neglect-
ing existing customs, of perfectionism, of not being interested enough in systematic thinking, of deprecating
the role of religious leadership and of not following the
authority of the ministerial office. All these criticisms
against Spener by Loescher are being made today with
some plausibility and legitimacy against the encounter
culture.[85]

The more we examine our subject, the more we are
astonished at the relatively unnoticed parallel between
hasidic Judaism and Protestant pietism. It is amazing
that the lives of John Wesley and Israel ben Eliezer (the
Baal Shem-Tob) are so similar in so many particulars.
The Baal Shem-Tob, or Master of The Good Name, the
founder of Hasidism, was born about 1700, John Wesley,
founder of Methodism, in 1703. Both had legends associated with their births. Each had a father who led a
pious and religiously disciplined life. Both were fascinated by the emotive power of their religious tradition
but felt that power to be unactualized in its bequeathed
forms, which were too rigid to grasp the deeper truth
of the tradition they were trying to mediate.

In his thirty-sixth year, while Wesley was preaching
in Georgia, the Baal Shem made himself known as a char-

ismatic teacher and healer and inaugurated a widespread revival of Jewish religious life. Shortly thereafter (1738) John Wesley returned from Georgia to inaugurate the profound renewal of English church life known as the evangelical revival.

Both Wesley and the Baal Shem were interested in the body and its healing. The Baal Shem had studied the healing properties of herbs, while reading the teachings of the great masters of Kabala and the Zohar. Wesley compiled a book of *Physic,* which cataloged many medical remedies for lay usage, and which was widely circulated on the American frontier. Not surprisingly, the Baal Shem and Wesley both elicited hostility from the medical profession for their intrusions into medical territory (just as today there is a great deal of anxiety and criticism from the medical profession toward the encounter culture). The Baal Shem went much farther than Wesley in his fascination with the occult, telepathy, and prophecy. Wesley was more cautious about the ecstatic, the quietistic, and the mystical.[86] But both men created popular movements that sought to deepen and democratize religious experiencing. The Baal Shem sought to spread the knowledge of the Kabala to the people so that all might understand the revelation which rabbinic leadership thought should be reserved only for the elite few. Similarly Wesley, as a prototype of British pietism, offended Anglican sensibilities by claiming, "The world is my parish" and by preaching in the fields to the displaced persons of the industrial revolution.[87]

One explanatory note is due to Roman Catholic readers of this chapter. Much more attention needs to be given by historical scholars to the relationship between Roman Catholic developments (in the tradition of Loyola, St. Theresa, Madame Guyon, and Fénelon) and the Protestant and Jewish sources of which I am speaking here. This is a neglected area of historical scholarship. The study of Protestant pietism has proceeded relatively independently in relation to Roman Catholic and Jewish sources of that period. It will be evident to Catholic readers that my thesis limits itself principally to developing the analogies between current encounter and its Jewish and Protestant precedents. This is not to deny that Roman Catholic patterns had a similar role to play, but at this point the historical scholarship is too incomplete for the development of that view. I would certainly encourage its further investigation. When I developed my thesis I was working principally in my own area of competence, viz., the Protestant theological tradition. But through association with my colleague Will Herberg and others, it became increasingly evident to me that the hasidic tradition directly parallels Protestant pietism in astonishing ways that were more evident than parallels in the Roman tradition. So I focus on Jewish and Protestant sources, but without any implication that Catholic sources were not similarly influential and perhaps very powerfully so. I can only invite Catholic scholars and others to develop further the thesis I am presenting in terms of the rich tradition of Roman Catholic piety of the seventeenth, eighteenth, and nineteenth centuries.[88]

No better conclusion to this section may be found than to note, by way of summary, the six basic assumptions that Sam Keen says are fundamental for the "soft revolution." [89] It should not be surprising, even though Keen does not seem to notice it, that each of these assumptions is deeply engrained in eighteenth-century pietism: (1) "Religion is not a matter of belonging to any organization, but one of a *new form of consciousness*," says Keen of the "soft revolution." Likewise religion, in the tradition of pietism, was equally a revolt against formalism and a search for a new religious consciousness. It was Schleiermacher who finally gave theological plausibility to this pietistic insight. (2) Nothing could be more characteristic of pietism than Keen's second characterization of the "soft revolution": viz., "it is possible to have *a direct transcendental experience of God*." That is what the evangelical revivals and hasidic piety were all about. (3) "Religious consciousness may be cultivated by such disciplines as yoga, meditation, chanting, dancing, divination . . . and the study of ancient religious texts." Likewise we find in pietism a persistent concern for the *disciplining* of the religious life in ways that clearly parallel these prevailing disciplines, with crucial focus on the control and ordering of body functioning as an aspect of religious growth. (4) "The true power to change society must come from the individual who is fully sensual and lives his beliefs." The hunger for full sensory immersion in religious experience, for deep emotive involvement and radical appropriation of the religious life, is a well-known keystone of Protestant and Jewish pietism. The hope that the *larger social organism would be transformed by such renewed persons* may be seen in the social reform movements spawned by pietism, such as abolitionism and the "social gospel." [90] (5) *"Experience and experimentation* rather than authority and revelation are the foundations of religion." I cannot agree with Keen that the soft revolution is without its own hunger for revelation, as may be seen from *Hair* to *Jesus Christ Superstar* and the Jesus

People.[91] In any event, crucial to pietistic faith as well as to the soft revolution is the focus upon "experience and experimentation" rather than authoritarian and rigid scholastic concepts of revelation.[92] Wesley spoke of his societies as an effort in "experimental religion." (6) "Many strange things may be true—E.S.P., astrology, magic—so it is best to keep an open mind." Like the soft revolution, the pietistic movement was drawn to the occult, to psychic phenomena, to healings and miraculous interventions, and an experimental attitude toward transpersonal phenomena.[93] In each case, the basic features of the "soft revolution" are anticipated by innovators in small experimental religious societies of the eighteenth century.

5. THE MEDIUM (GROUP ENCOUNTER) IS THE MASSAGE

When Marshall McLuhan says, "The medium is the massage," he means that the form through which men communicate decisively shapes what is communicated. "Societies have always been shaped more by the nature of the media by which men communicate than by the content of the communication." [94] McLuhan has persuasively shown that we no longer live in a world of visual, linear, rational, sequential communication. Interpersonal encounter is more credible as a medium of communication than are sequential arguments in books and essays.[95] As a result of media changes, we are coming into a new era of primitive, tribal oral communication. The tribal environment is basically a tactile and auditory environment. It is being reawakened through the media revolution. We are experiencing the "orientalization of the West by electric technology. . . . Other cultures, native and Oriental, have been developed on quite different sensory plans, for not only is each sense a unique world, but it offers unique pleasures and pains. . . . Civilization is entirely the product of phonetic literacy, and as it dissolves with the electronic revolution, we rediscover a tribal, integral awareness that manifests itself in a complete shift in our sensory lives." [96]

Utilizing McLuhan's language and categories, we now ask, What is the *medium* used in Protestant pietistic encounter and how does it compare with the medium of the current encounter culture? In both cases, the medium is clearly the same: oral communication in a small-group scale, involving tactile processes and the entire sensorium in personal growth and conversion.

Pietism never produced a respected theological literature. Speculative theology was less fascinating to it than live small-group encounter. What kind of literature did pietism produce? A literature that looks and "feels" much like the literature of current encounter culture. It was a literature of devotion and exhortation, of technique and practical behavioral change, of experimental mysticism and fascination with the occult. Its failure to produce a viable tradition of academic theology is paralleled by the failure of current encounter culture to produce a corpus of theoretical literature that would equal in impressiveness its actual innovative spirit.[97]

Most historians of Christian thought have been immensely bored by pietism. The chief reason is that pietism has produced such a negligible amount of "systematic theology." What it did produce was an astonishing variety of communities experimenting with religious encounter, integrating faith into the whole of life. Since pietism itself was an experimental theology, there was a steady resistance to the very attempt to write any final or systematic presentation of theological systems, partly because it knew that whatever was written soon would have to be rewritten in the light of new experiencing. This is equally characteristic of the encounter culture with its lack of interest in systematic theorizing.

The principal medium of communication for both pietism and the encounter culture is *the here and now verbal encounter in a small-group context with a high level of mutual trust*. The medium is talk—experience-based talk, and that in small groups, with a strong emotive and experiential focus. It is not the academic treatise. It is not surprising that the academic establishment has been among the last to become interested in encounter techniques (despite their relevance for the educational process) just as academia was slow in seeing any value in pietistic radicalism.

The movement spawned by Moreno, Lewin, Rogers, Perls, Maslow, and Benne could not have occurred without the available models of societal interaction derived from the Judeo-Christian tradition. Over against the popular view that the religious inspiration of the encounter culture comes from Eastern religions, I am convinced that the basic "I-thou" model of interpersonal encounter was delivered to the encounter culture from Jewish theologians such as Buber and from Protestant thinkers such as Kierkegaard, Tillich, and Gogarten long before they became common currency in existential philosophy. The encounter model is only awkwardly and unconvincingly attributed to Hindu and Buddhist thought. This is not to idealize the West. Much that the encounter culture is protesting is a result of basic inadequacies in Western society. But its protest is as Western as the Western distortions against which it is protesting.

We conclude this historical chapter with the recollection that 1975 will be the three-hundredth year or tercentenary, for the birth of Protestant pietism, since Spener's *Pia desideria* appeared in 1675 in Frankfurt. It seems appropriate that some special note be made of this occasion, especially since the pietistic movement is very much alive today in demythologized and secularized forms, even though it has been largely neglected and abused by those who have been powerfully influenced by it.[98]

Chapter Three

GROUP TRUST
AND ULTIMATE TRUST

What is the implicit theology at work in the human potential movement? Despite rejections of traditional theology, the human potential movement [1] has its own quasi-official, implicit theology. Its apostolic tradition is handed down from the "saints," fervently believed by those who are susceptible to belief, and enthusiastically propagated by missionaries committed to "the evangelization of the world in this generation." [2]

This chapter constitutes the heart of our effort to deal seriously with the encounter culture as a demythologized, secularized Judeo-Christian theology.[3] In attempting to develop a theological interpretation of the encounter culture, we will probe four issues:

1. What are the implicit assumptions about the nature of reality as accepting and trustworthy that operate in group encounter, and how do they relate to the proclamation of the Christian community concerning the self-disclosure of the accepting reality? My hypothesis is that the trusting environment of a group with a high trust level is based not merely upon the experience of being trusted by persons but upon the deeper assumption that

the cosmic environment is itself in a primordial sense trustworthy.

2. How has the Biblical witness anticipated much current talk about body language? Nonverbal communication is, to a very large extent, the language of God's self-disclosure. We will inquire into the possibility of a nonverbal theology, or a theology of nonverbal communication.

3. Does the operational structure of encounter theology demonstrate an implicit understanding of the human predicament, the redemptive process, and corporate accountability parallel to the Judeo-Christian tradition?

4. Why has academic theology remained aloof and uninterested in the exciting developments in the intensive group process in the last decade? We will try to understand the particular malaise of contemporary theology that up to now has prevented an open and critical engagement with these important developments in the behavioral sciences and popular religion.

1. THE IMPLICIT ONTOLOGICAL ASSUMPTIONS OF GROUP TRUST

The following working definitions will help us clarify the boundaries of our discussion: By *theology* we mean the deliberate attempt to make internally consistent the self-understanding that lives in response to the witness of the Christian community to God's self-revelation in history. By *intensive group experience* we mean any group of persons whose interpersonal transactions exhibit a high degree of congruence, openness, honesty, intimacy, and straightforward feedback. By *ontological* we mean that which pertains to the nature of being itself. An *ontological assumption* is an assumption about being, or the ground of being. An *implicit ontological assumption* refers to that which we assume about being itself which, even though we are not explicit about articulating it consciously, we nonetheless presuppose to be a prevailing relationship that all beings have with the source and ground of being. *Christ* is the expected deliverer, the fulfillment of human hopes. *Kerygma* is the announcement of the good news that Jesus is the Christ. *Koinonia* refers to the community or fellowship that emerges and exists in response to the love of God in Jesus Christ, which expresses in limited ways the communion or fellowship that God has, *de jure,* with all humanity.

Ours is no idle question: Is it possible for the Christian community appropriately to understand the basic encounter group as an indirect expression of Christian faith and community? Many Christian educators have experienced the intensive group process so positively as to imply that there must be some analogy with the community that Christians know in Jesus Christ. Yet few would wish to reduce Christian community to T-groups or encounter processes.

I do not find exceptionally convincing the view that non-Christians cannot achieve as deep and intimate a group encounter as can Christians. It seems all too clear that in the so-called secular setting, without religious language, group processes can be extremely effective in creating profound levels of trust and a quality of interpersonal openness and care which looks very much like Christian koinonia.

The difference between Christian encounter and secular encounter is that in Christian encounter Jesus is celebrated and known as the Christ, the fulfillment of human hopes. In secular encounter God's love is present incognito, received indirectly but not confessed.

It may seem inconsistent to say on the one hand that secular encounter is able to actualize genuine human community at least in fragmented ways and then to turn around and make claims about a deeper sense of community which is possible only in response to God's community-granting love. The question itself must be reformulated, however, if it should be the case that God's love exists incognito amid the intensive secular encounter.

God's love does not need to be recognized by us in order to be present in us. God's word does not need to be spoken by our lips in order to be addressed to our concrete situations. God's redemptive action does not need to be confessed by us in order to be at work in our human transactions. When God's love, word, and redemptive action are appropriately recognized, spoken, and confessed by men, however, they better understand the ground upon which they already stand.

Is trust a response to the trustworthiness of God, or is trust a response to the trustworthiness of other human beings? This is the crux of the theological dilemma. We are not inconsistent in saying that the most profound trust is known only in the self-disclosing trustworthiness of God in Jesus Christ, yet this same trustworthiness is opaquely reflected through the trustworthiness of other human beings.

How can an intensive group experience that assumes that ordinary human beings, without any recognized relation to God's revelation, have the capacity to share trust, care, and intimacy be consistent with the Christian understanding of community that beholds the natural man in a radical estrangement from himself and others which can be overcome only through the infinite forgiving love of God?

The proposal that seems most hopeful in offering a solution to this seeming inconsistency follows: In all effective group encounter, there is at work a hidden and tacit ontological assumption, i.e., an assumption about the nature of being itself.[4] It is assumed that it is not merely persons who are the source of interpersonal acceptance but that the ground of being itself is accepting. It is on the basis of this awareness of the acceptance of reality itself that we mediate acceptance to one another. The trusting environment of a group with a high trust level is not based solely on the experience of being trusted by persons. Rather, it operates at the much deeper level of understanding the cosmic environment as trustworthy. This cosmic acceptance may not be articulated, but it is profoundly felt and mediated through persons. In an effective group one experiences both interpersonal trust and the ontological ground upon which interpersonal trust is based. The group that cannot experience reality as trustable is not probing the depths of group trust.[5]

At the cost of possible repetition, let me try to say this in slightly different language: No group member or combination of members is ultimately the source of the deepest acceptance experienced in the trusting group. The trusting member only points to an acceptance that has its source beyond the group. The group is not finally the deepest wellspring of trust. Its trust points beyond itself to a deeper trustworthiness that is written into reality itself, and without an awareness of this, the group does not function as optimally helpful.

As evidence for this assumption, let us examine the way in which a group deals with a person who experiences anxiety and guilt. The group tries to convey to the individual that there is no need in reality itself to be guilty or anxious. The group implicitly assumes that the individual does not know himself truly when he does not trust fully his own awareness continuum, when he is distrustful of the future, and when he cannot open himself to his experiencing.[6] This assumption is much more profound in its philosophical implication than is ordinarily acknowledged by the group.

The next step of our argument is that it is this implicit assumption of the trustworthiness of reality itself which is in fact made explicit in the Christian kerygma, which announces that God has taken the initiative in addressing history with his infinite forgiving love, and making himself known as trustworthy. So in a sense the group performs a representative ministry, trying to get through to persons in the group that they can trust others because here and now reality is trustable, that they need not be radically guilty, that they can be open with others, that they can accept themselves since they are in fact accepted. Accepted by what? Not finally by the group itself, but by some principle intrinsic to the creation itself.

It is in this way that the intensive group process is unconsciously related to a theology of Christian community. For the very ground of trust that is implicitly presupposed in the secular group experience is made explicit in the Christian proclamation of God's self-disclosing love.

What, then, constitutes the basic difference between

the secular group experience and Christian koinonia? Only that the latter has learned to make explicit the trust that is implicit in the former. The uniqueness of Christian koinonia is that here, from time to time, the word of God's acceptance is announced not merely as an idea in our heads but as an *event* in which we share. The trustworthiness of God is known not because we have an idea of his trustworthiness but because he has made himself known as trustworthy through Christ. The trustworthy reality that the group may vaguely experience is explicitly celebrated in Christian worship as a trust that has made itself known in history.[7]

It is indeed important for persons to experience themselves in a trustworthy environment, but that says very little about the deeper nature of the trustworthiness of being itself. The Christian proclamation does in fact speak of the trustworthiness of being itself, not on the basis of the bare idea of the trustworthiness of being, but on the basis of a history in which being itself is making itself known as trustworthy. The self-disclosure of the trustworthiness of being is what the gospel is all about. This eventful story is remembered in Christian worship. Failure to grasp this explicit/implicit relationship has deprived both theolgy and group encounter of the possibility of joining in a mutually beneficial dialogue.

If it should be the case that secular intensive group processes can experience to a considerable degree the same kind of trusting relationships that are present in authentic Christian koinonia, then what is the point of talking about Christian koinonia? Why preach if the trust that is present in Jesus Christ is hidden in the intensive group experience? A very similar question is faced in the New Testament when Paul speaks of the fact that there is no distinction between Jew and Greek. The same Lord is Lord of all, and he sows his riches upon all who call upon him (Rom. 10:12). It then becomes necessary for Paul to show why the church must proclaim the gospel. The purpose of proclamation, he says, is to *help men to come into an awareness of the situation in which they always already exist,* namely, into the presence of God's trustworthiness. Proclamation is not intended to introduce God to the world as if he were not already there. Preachers do not create the trustworthiness of God. They merely introduce man to the reality in which he already stands. Paul asks: How are they to believe in Him of whom they have never heard? How are they to hear without a preacher? Faith comes from what is heard, and what is heard comes by the preaching of Christ (Rom. 10:17).

Admittedly a diffuse awareness of the trustworthiness of being itself can be mediated through interpersonal relationships without the kerygma, i.e., without the church's specific witness to the self-disclosure of God in history. It is not necessary for groups to become overtly kerygmatic in order to experience that trust. The kerygma, however, does complete a circle that is begun by the intensive group experience.

It may become important at certain moments in the group's life together to announce the word of God's trustworthiness clearly. But always that word deserves to be clarified in the language of the individual to whom it is addressed, instead of just being imposed as if from the outside of his awareness continuum.

It should not be surprising that a group that understands itself as consciously responding to God's covenant love might from time to time more adequately embody that love and trust than a group in which that awareness is not fully present. There may indeed be times in a secular group when it is appropriate to talk about the forgiving, suffering love of God in Jesus Christ. Even there it should never be forgotten that the trustworthiness of God can be communicated without language. The cross, for example, is a word event that is spoken nonverbally through an occurrence.

Why should not persons who are serious about small groups give careful attention to the Christian witness to the self-disclosure of the trustworthiness of reality itself? In other words, why should not this specific kerygmatic witness be made by the church to the encounter group? Indeed this witness deserves to be made, but it is a bit too obvious to say merely that the Christian community wants to communicate the kerygma. Rather more deeply the Christian community is free to join with secular groups in celebration of the trustworthiness and love of God that is powerfully present incognito precisely amid the secular group! The more difficult insight to grasp is the affirmation of the Christian community that the trustworthiness of God is present in the midst of human relationships that may be totally unaware of his trustworthiness.[8]

We wish specifically to avoid the introversion which claims that the only authentic encounter is that which is experienced by those who hear the kerygma. To be sure, those who hear the kerygma have the richer possibility of receiving Christ's community in a larger frame of reference. Yet those who live in Christ make an affirmation about secular group processes that these processes may not want to say or cannot say: the ground of their trust is made known in history in Jesus Christ.

There is a profound sense, then, in which the intensive group experience may be an incognito expression of Christian koinonia.

2. NONVERBAL COMMUNICATION AND A THEOLOGY OF HAPPENINGS

A widespread phenomenon is occurring in the encounter culture—the deciphering of the language of the nonverbal. Groups learn to watch for how the body is speaking. Building on the tradition of Reich, Perls, and Lowen, they unravel the code of body language. Our bodies broadcast accurately much truth about who we are as persons.[9]

Experimenting with nonverbal communication is a major concern of the encounter culture. Group games in nonverbal communication seek to reveal how we communicate to each other through gesturing, touching, withdrawing, fidgeting, grimacing, etc. It is often found that more important messages are communicated without words than with them, and often more forcefully.

What meaning do such experiments have for Christian education and Christian worship? What special contribution might the Christian tradition make to the analysis of nonverbal communication.[10]

The interest of the encounter culture in event language and body language has profound precedent in the Biblical witness. The precedent does not lie merely at the surface level of royal pageantry or clothing or seasonal celebrations or ritual gesturing, although indeed all of these are nonverbal communications. The deepest analogy is to be found in the Christian celebration of the incarnate love of God. When God addresses us with his once-for-all message to human history, it is not in the form of an epistle, or a treatise on ethics, but by his own embodiment of the message, by his own sharing in human existence, illustrating what it is to love, by himself being one who loves.

At the heart of the liturgy are the words of institution: "This is my body given for you, take and eat in remembrance of me." [11] It is God's own self-giving through his body, symbolically re-presented. This has a sexual analogy, inasmuch as a sexual partner offers his body to the beloved for enjoyment and celebration of the flesh. Surely we receive a penetrating message from the Christian liturgy about the importance of body language. The liturgical act is itself a meal in which the body is being fed. Christ is embodying himself to us and being incorporated into our bodies.

Under the conditions of human estrangement, we use our bodies defensively, according to Wilhelm Reich, to help brace us against anxieties and guilt. Muscles work to help us resist feelings. We use our bodies as armor.[12] Reich's view may be related to the classical Christian picture of the radical fallenness of man, in which man is alienated from his own body. He cannot feel his feelings (cf. Rogers on incongruence).

In the midst of man's incongruence and body alienation comes good news that God himself shares in human history by taking the form of human flesh. The incarnation is about God's becoming a human form, a body. God shares in our condition. The Word becomes flesh. When God speaks his word, he speaks through events. Biblical theology is a theology of happenings. The verbal accumulation called theology is always a secondary reflection on *events* such as the imprisonment of a nation or a crucifixion. The Biblical saga of the exodus is secondary to the event itself. The theology that follows remembers the event, celebrates it, reappropriates it, but does not create it. A modest theology will not forget the event character of God's address.

It is precisely here that Christian theology can join in dialogue with the most far-out nonverbal experimentation. It can say to the encounter culture, we too have long been concerned with body language, so much so that when Christianity begins to speak of the suffering of God, it speaks of the body language of God's suffering, the cross. When it speaks of deliverance, it speaks of an event, the exodus. Whereas much popular religion is narrowly concerned with *ideas* about God and religion, the Biblical witness remains more concerned with *events* in which the truth is historically embodied.

McLuhan has shown that the Protestant tradition is decisively shaped by print media. By contrast, the larger stream of Judeo-Christian worship has utilized multimedia dramaturgical communication to carry the weight of this tradition into the present.[13]

The systems of communication in the Biblical witness are not fundamentally linear or sequential arguments. We accept too readily the systematic and linear conception of communication through print media as normative. So when we try to listen to the Bible, we want to transform it into a systematic ethical treatise. But the systems of communication in the Biblical witness involved a complex web of nonverbal communications such as the laying on of hands, the washing of feet, the breaking of bread, the driving of money changers out of the Temple. Much new Biblical study needs to be done on the nature of that nonverbal communication system and its relevance for us. If we do that job well, we will see many more analogies between the Biblical witness and the encounter culture. Sensate experiencing and symbolic body language were central to those communication systems.

What is being expressed nonverbally, for example, when Jesus washes the feet of his disciples? Through body language he is saying to them (here the verbal supplements the nonverbal act): "A new commandment I give to you, that you love one another; even as I have loved you, that you also love one another" (John 13:34 ff.).

What kind of interpersonal transaction is occurring when we experience the passing of the peace? Hands touch hands, moving around the circle of community, expressing the *shalom* of God amid human estrangement.

What is communicated nonverbally in an act of pilgrimage? As an act of devotion the believer takes himself bodily to the holy place, bodily bespeaking his adoration and confession, putting his whole body into the process of confessing and petitioning, as when he moves step by step through the stations of the cross.

What is the body language of baptism? A life is being cleansed by going under water, symbolically saying that one is dying to an old understanding of life. He then emerges out of that death as a new man, committed to life in response to the grace of God.

One means by which Jesus chose to announce his messianic ministry was by performing acts of healing as a sign of the coming reign of God. The lame walk, the blind see, the dumb speak. Bodies are transformed in

the presence of the messianic person. The announcement of the coming reign of God is made not only with
words but also with healing actions.

All of the force of nonverbal communication is cul-
minated and symbolized in the eucharistic action, where
people sit at a meal together. Bread is eaten and wine
received as a participation in the brokenness of Christ
for us. We engage in a bodily act, sharing in God's own
bodily self-giving on our behalf.

The same concern for nonverbal communication may
be seen in the Old Testament, where the verbal supplements the live transverbal happening of God's judgment and love. The important thing about the exodus
is not that Yahweh delivers a discourse about deliverance, but that he acts so as to deliver a nation from
bondage. When Yahweh judges Israel, he does not
merely say, "You are judged," but says it through a
judging event, captivity in Babylon. The Hebraic style
of communication is steeped in body language: touching,
embracing, gesturing, kissing, dancing.[14]

We conclude this section with a remarkable story
from Luke's Gospel: "And behold, a woman of the city,
who was a sinner, when she learned that he [Jesus] was
sitting at table in the Pharisee's house, brought an ala-
baster flask of ointment, and standing behind him at his
feet, weeping, she began to wet his feet with her tears,
and wiped them with the hair of her head, and kissed
his feet, and anointed them with the ointment." (Luke
7:37–38.) When the Pharisee began to complain that
if Jesus were a prophet, he would not let this sort of
woman touch him, Jesus answered: "Do you see this
woman? I entered your house, you gave me no water
for my feet, but she has wet my feet with her tears and

wiped them with her hair. You gave me no kiss, but from the time I came in she has not ceased to kiss my feet. You did not anoint my head with oil, but she has anointed my feet with ointment. Therefore, I tell you, her sins, which are many, are forgiven, for she loved much; but he who is forgiven little, loves little." (Vs. 44–47.)

3. THE STRUCTURE OF ENCOUNTER THEOLOGY

Despite its rejection of traditional "official" theology, the encounter culture expresses an *implicit* theology that secularizes the basic categories of the Judeo-Christian tradition. In order to grasp the implicit theology of encounter groups, we must first clarify a tripartite structure of all human experiencing that is reflected in all well-formed theological thinking.

Among persons whom I have come to know well, I have found them always to be struggling with three fundamental human questions:

I	II	III
What are the limits of my being that frustrate my self-actualization?	What possibilities are open for deliverance from my predicament?	How can I actualize these possibilities in order to become more self-fulfilled?

No one whom I have come to know well has avoided asking these questions in some form. They belong to the structure of human existence.

Effective *psychotherapy*, regardless of theoretical orientation, is similarly concerned to grapple with (1) the blockages, bondage, limitations, conflicts, guilt, and anxieties that limit human fulfillment and frustrate self-actualization; (2) opening up possibilities for deliverance from those blockages and envisioning the fully functioning person; and (3) the reshaping of behavior into a fuller expression of this envisioned possibility and the implementation of behavioral change.

This same threefold sequence is expressed in Christian *worship* in the form of the acts of:

Confession   Thanksgiving   Commitment

That is to say, the worshiping community gathers (1) to acknowledge its bondage, sin, limitation, and inadequacy; (2) to celebrate the good news of God's delivering action; and (3) to commit itself to the reshaping of life in accordance with this renewing possibility. The essence of Christian worship is the movement of a community of faith through this sequence of three acts, the absence of any one of which would leave the community lopsided and fragmented.

Three questions, likewise, are the explicit concern of any well-integrated *theology:* (1) What is man's predicament? (2) How has God acted to deliver man from his predicament? (3) What is the appropriate response of man to God's action? Thus Christian worship and theology speak to issues that are embedded in the existence of every man. Theology is the servant of the worshiping and witnessing community. The purpose of theology is to order the self-understanding of this community into a self-consistent whole in the light of Scriptural truth experienced in life and illuminated by reason and tradition. Any theology that fails to deal with these three elemental human concerns is diluted and stunted.

Alternative ways of expressing this threefold structure familiar to any integral theology are as follows:

THE WORLD'S NEED	GOD'S ACTION	THE CHURCH'S RESPONSE
Bondage	Deliverance	Mission
Sin	Grace	Responsibility
Guilt	Justification	Sanctification
Creation	Redemption	Consummation
God the Father	God the Son	God the Holy Spirit
The human predica-ment	The gospel	The life of faith

It shall be our purpose in this section to show that the intensive group experience, when it is operating at its most effective level, is dealing with this same sequence of issues.

a. The Human Predicament

Despite much talk in the human potential movement of the highly exalted possibilities of man, there is none-theless a powerful stress on human estrangement, and a practical effort to identify its nature, dynamics, and viciousness. It should not surprise us that a high doc-trine of man's possibility is linked with a radical concept of human alienation, since that is precisely the pattern we have seen operative in the Judeo-Christian tradition from the Hebrew prophets through Jesus, Paul, Augus-tine, and the Reformation. In fact, it can be persuasively argued that it is only where the human potentiality is taken most seriously that it is even possible to develop a depth understanding of human estrangement.

It may seem strange that precisely the movement that so often quotes William James on the incalculably high human potentiality would also be the same movement that is frequently criticized for being so rough on participants, too critical and faultfinding, too ready to show man's intransigent alienation.[15] Yet this is a familiar dialectic in the mainstream of Western religious thought: to behold man's vast human potential simultaneously juxtaposed with his radical alienation.

There is in the encounter culture a strongly held (demythologized Christian) assumption that the original, natural human being is fundamentally good in his deepest intentionality. His organismic valuing process as a child is trustable (Rogers), i.e., the infant is thoroughly in touch with his feeling process and fully open to experiencing. There is no disjunction or incongruence between experiencing and symbolizing of experience. There is in infant experiencing a full, free flow of energy that is not blocked by "introjected values" which do not coincide with the actual experiencing process. There is an innate self-actualizing tendency (Horney) which, however violated or distorted it may be, nonetheless seeks to move the human organism toward its own good.[16] This tendency is repeatedly appealed to in the intensive group process and relied upon as the fundamental resource for change in all participants.

Although there is a strong affirmation of man's innate tendency toward self-actualization, there is at the same time in group encounter a powerful determination to reveal and deal with alienation. Man is estranged from his own deeper feeling levels. The fall of man is a fall away from his original capacity for open experiencing. In transactional terms, the fall of man occurs with the introjection of "parent" voices in such a way that the "adult" (rational data-receiving capacity) becomes "contaminated" and the "child" cannot express itself fully.

Not only does the encounter culture have its own version of man's radical fallenness but it also may be said to have reappropriated the Augustinian notion of original sin in its general acceptance of the Freudian theory that the culture or societal matrix of superego forces *inevitably* tyrannizes the ego and the id so that we may always expect from human societies the element of repressiveness.[17]

The radicality of man's predicament, however, is taken a step farther by group encounter in a way that appears to be a secularized version of the Pauline-Augustinian-Lutheran *bondage of the will*. The malignant character of the human predicament is seen in the fact that man is alienated at such a depth that he does not even recognize his alienation. He is blind to his blindness. He is self-deceptive to the degree that he is often totally unaware of his self-deception. He is locked into body dysfunctioning that is a muscular response to his anxieties and guilts, and his anxieties and guilts are reinforced by his locked-up body. He tries desperately to prevent himself and others from recognizing the depth character of his self-deceptions. Thus the group must work hard to bring him to the point where he is able to listen to feedback about his dysfunctioning. Much of the group's effort is devoted to penetrating these defenses to reveal the pernicious character of his self-deception. The dynamics of these defenses are profoundly anticipated and analyzed in the Judeo-Christian understanding of the bondage of the will.

Although the encounter culture would certainly wish to avoid traditional terms such as original sin, the fall of Adam, and the bondage of the will, it seems evident that the encounter culture is searching for existential equivalents to these concepts through their analyses of guilt, impotence, self-deception, depression, withdrawal, etc. All these terms are descriptive of the deeper intention of the Judeo-Christian view of man's radical alienation from himself, others, and the ground of his life.

b. Redemption

There is an implicit doctrine of redemption in the encounter culture which assumes that when persons are in genuine contact with each other, open to their here and now experiencing process, and accepting of each other, then positive change will occur and they will in some measure find release from the predicament we have described. Salvation in this sense, from the Latin *salvus* (meaning health), is mediated interpersonally, not through a professional elite but through a community of ordinary people. It is mediated not through ideas but through *relationships* that enable persons to overcome that demonic power of anxiety and guilt. What changes people is not mere cognitive knowledge of their predicament, but entering into a new relationship in which they know themselves to be positively valued by others beyond their negative behaviors and accepted without conditions of worth.

What saves is not the technical expertise or diagnostic capacity or analytical ability of the participants, but rather their capacity to enter into the frame of reference of their neighbors and communicate authentic accepting care and love. If congruence, empathy, and unconditional positive regard are not present, growth should not be expected. What is important is not the *idea* of the value of persons, or the concept of the infinite worth of the human self, but rather a *relationship* in which persons experience themselves as unconditionally valued by others.

Christian faith celebrates a "redemptive process" at work in the intensive group experience, quite apart from any overt religious language. Participants may experience a kind of death and rebirth. They are being offered the possibility of dying to their old self-understanding and of being born anew. In the midst of this new human environment of trust, accountability, and mutual support, they discover possibilities of self-fulfillment that were not present within the context of estrangement.

How does this happen? It happens when ordinary human beings listen to others in their lostness, share empathetically in the depth of their alienation, communicate that sharing authentically, provide them with accurate descriptive feedback on how they are being experienced, and above all help them to recognize that they are accepted precisely in the midst of their alienation. The most feared possibilities and the most guilt-ridden memories are able to be received without "conditions of worth" being placed upon the relationship. They learn to value themselves anew because they have been valued anew by others.

The group in effect takes the hand of the person and descends with him into his hell of fear, despair, hatred, or helplessness. The group is not like a professional therapist who is paid to do diagnostic work. Part of the reason why the group may be more effective is that its service is a gift.

Since the encounter group ordinarily does not use overtly religious symbols, it might seem that there is little point in trying to compare Christian salvation with encounter group growth. We are not saying that they are the same. God's saving action is not the same as persons facilitating others' growth. Rather, we are saying that there is an implicit theology of a saving relationship in the encounter group which is in some ways analogous to the saving event of which Christian proclamation speaks. Each dimension of the redemptive process in group encounter has Christological analogies: incarnation, eschatological healing, pardon, judgment, death, and resurrection.

c. Self-actualization

The final phase of any theological inquiry asks how human behavior is reshaped in response to the redemptive possibility. Christ comes—So what? How does the saving event become a saving event for me, to the depths of my being, and for the reshaping of my existence?

These same questions are probed in a secularized fashion in the encounter group, which is concerned with moving the self toward a fuller actualization of the possibility given in the redemptive group. In terms of traditional theological language, we are speaking of growing in grace, or in response to the gracious action of God through the guidance of the Spirit, and of movement toward more perfect love.[18] How does the "convert" appropriate the saving event in his behavior? How does he grasp the redemptive possibility so that it can be truly manifest in his daily growth?

Continuing to experience the judgment and love of the group, persons grow in their capacity to stay in the here and now, experience a freer flow of feelings and speech, own up to their irresponsible behavior, experience less blockage in internal dialogue. They learn to symbolize their experiences more adequately through continued participation as "communicants" in a "growth-producing community." Through this continued nurturing they learn more fully to trust their own feeling processes, so that new contexts are experienced with greater immediacy.

Just as in the Catholic and Protestant traditions there is a goal of perfect love as the *telos,* or end, of the conversion process, or of radical responsiveness to the address of God (cf. Bultmann's "radical obedience" or Wesley's "perfect love" or Bonhoeffer's "formation in Christ"), so are these same notions recapitulated in a demythologized sense in the encounter group with its notions of radical personal accountability, of being fully open to one's experiencing, of being sensitive to others, of being a person in process, and of being fully able to enter into relationships of intimacy (cf. Rogers' "fully functioning person," Jourard's "self-disclosing person," Perls's "here and now" existence, Berne's "adult").

We have shown how the encounter process embodies an implicit theology that unconsciously has its roots in the Judeo-Christian understanding of the human predicament, the redemptive process, and the responsive life of faith. Now we turn to ask about the current condition of studies in theology, and why they have resisted a fuller development of this dialogue.

4. THE INCREDIBLE BOREDOM OF THEOLOGY IN THE PRESENCE OF THE ENCOUNTER CULTURE

Before leaving our theme, that of a theological interpretation of the intensive group process, we must not neglect some needed observations on why theology has remained so remarkably aloof and uninterested, even bored, with these important developments during the past decade. One might reasonably expect theologians to be keenly interested in a vast popular movement in search of religious experience.[19] Especially after suffering the "death of God" episode, one might even expect theologians to be moderately intrigued by the renewed popular interest in the direct experience of God, in meditation, in transpersonal awareness, and in psychic phenomena. It is all the more surprising then to realize that theologians generally not only have dismissed and ignored the encounter culture as if it did not exist but also have responded generally with defensiveness and aloofness to any suggestion that it might be theologically important. Theologians have been uncommonly happy to leave the intensive group experience to the pastoral counselors, religious educators, group workers, and church administrators.

We are now in a stage of radical experimentation in the encounter culture far different from the tamer time of the invention of T-groups and the heyday of "group dynamics." Already we are beginning to see a strong negative reaction against many of the fanatical tendencies of the encounter process. Yet the church, despite its obvious investment in this dialogue, has generally counted itself out. The issues have been joined, but no theologians are present. After a long history of interest in small-group processes, just at the crucial moment the dialogue has been abandoned by theologians.

Ironically this abandonment has come just at a time when many of the encounter facilitators are seeking to discover themselves as religious beings. At a time when the encounter culture looks longingly toward Eastern religions for inspiration, little effort is being made by Christian or Jewish theologians to address the encounter culture with their own religious roots, which in point of fact have been so decisively important to the development of small-group encounter.

So preoccupied has theology been with its own internal stresses and with intricate linguistic and philosophical issues that it has seemed to have no energy for this demanding dialogue. Theology's recent concerns with apocalyptic, with hermeneutics, and with the ethics of war and revolution have left it psychologically at a great distance from the encounter culture.

What, then, is the unfortunate situation that prevails in academic theology which blinds it to the importance of group experimentation? Perhaps theology is afraid of opening a Pandora's box of eclectic fanaticism that it will not be able to control. Perhaps theology is afraid of the power of the Eastern religious resources that appear to be decisive in the encounter culture. Perhaps theology has had such a long and painful experience with the history of pietistic fanaticism and with theologies of "religious experience" that it simply does not have the heart or the nerve to tackle this potent, eclectic movement of secular religiosity.

Although these may be factors, a more subtle yet decisive reason for theology's suspicion of the encounter culture may be explained sociologically. It is to be found in theology's recent struggle to regain academic respectability in the university, a prestige that has steadily eroded for several decades, but never faster than in the late 1960's. Oddly enough, in this struggle, the academic study of religion has allowed itself to become firmly allied with forces in the academic establishment that generally are resistant to pedagogical innovation with group processes. Thus there are plausible, although not defensible, reasons for the aloofness of theology.

In the American university, theology has been struggling desperately to show the other university disciplines that it in fact does have a subject matter worth investigating. The academic study of religion has relied heavily upon careful historical studies as its principal method of achieving academic credentials. Historical, textual, and hermeneutical studies have been the most secure foothold that theology could gain in the university setting, which still nourishes many outmoded memories of the Enlightenment concerning the abuses of religion. Theology has in fact developed superb competencies in historical studies as a means of compensating for this steady polemic against the "sins of our fathers."

Yet, in the process of achieving these competencies in historical method, religious studies have paid the high price of losing touch with interpersonal processes, and with the concern for personal growth that has been such an important part of the pietistic tradition which is now being secularly renovated. That tradition has been a decided embarrassment to theology in gaining its academic credentials. Since Ritschl, the tradition of liberal theology has maintained a strong polemic against pietism. There remains today a heavy residue of many decades of polemic and tension between academic theology and the koinonaic concern of pietism.

Today's excellent religious scholar is often competent in the historical-critical analysis of his religious tradition, yet is embarrassed by his own actual religious community. He frequently comes on as strongly "parent" in transactional terms. His narrow focus on print media distracts him from sustained interpersonal encounter. In an age of nonlinear students, he remains doggedly committed to the linear argument. He can report about the *concept* of dialogue or "theologies of encounter" much better than he can live the life of dialogue, in Buber's sense.

So, regrettably, the excellent theological scholars of the past decade, whose expertise and brilliance is hardly questionable, are of a very different stripe from their fathers' or grandfathers' generation of theologians, who were more interpersonally involved, more pastoral in their outlook, more related to actual communities of worship and religious education, less introverted, more humane, and whose interests ranged much more broadly in interdisciplinary motifs.

A further reason for the boredom of theology with encounter is that theology has become strongly indebted to an elitist notion of the life of the mind, which runs strongly against the democratizing momentum of the encounter culture. This elitist self-conception is in turn closely related to the dependence of recent American theology upon the German academic model. During the decades 1945–1965, it was generally assumed in American theological circles that nothing was worth thinking unless it had been thought first in Germany. I know this well from personal experience, since I shared that assumption, carefully learned from my theological mentors—and, in fact, I selected German theologians (Bultmann and Barth) as foci for my dissertation, writing two books on German theological ethics before I became convinced that the American ethos had anything at all to offer theologically. Even today the principal voices in American theology still have their heads decisively turned toward German theology for their basic cues. Although most would give lip service to the need for an American theology, their operational style is still thoroughly German in character. That elitist stance, with all its brilliance, ingenuity, historical and analytical fastidiousness, has not been noteworthy for its respect for the humanizing resources of ordinary persons, nor has it been willing to venture much into nonauthoritarian pedagogies.[20]

Some of us who have attempted to go against that stream of elitism and have turned toward broad pedagogical experimentation utilizing the resources of the encounter culture, have felt the sting of criticism from our academic colleagues who feel that such a direction is soft-headed, bordering on fanaticism, and too willing to synthesize and embrace all manner of strange ideas and practices. Admitting that our direction does have its oddities and risks, we firmly believe that persons who still resolutely push the German academic model are riding on a sinking ship which the new student generation finds totally unconvincing. We no longer have the linear-oriented students to whom that model was relevant. In fact, the Germans students themselves are in hard rebellion against their own authoritarian system.

Students are demanding of professors that the professors be in touch with where the students themselves are interpersonally. The students want teaching to relate not just to their thought processes but to their whole human experience. Many students possess, as Postman and Weingartner say, "built-in automatic crap-detectors." They will not let the professors play their academic games. Students shaped by multiphased electronic media bombardment more than by books and linear arguments are unimpressed by the pretentious form of communication and scholarship to which most American theologians are deeply, perhaps irretrievably, committed.[21]

The same crisis that exists in theological education, of course, exists in other university disciplines. The reason why the crisis is especially critical in theology, however, is that no discipline in the American university has been more dependent and nostalgic than theology for the German academic pattern, which sharply intensifies the most undesirable features of the educational style against which the youth culture and the encounter culture currently are protesting.

If we must rebuild with a basically new pedagogy, how shall we begin? One way is to begin to risk a sustained dialogue with the syncretistic resources of the encounter culture, which has already dealt seriously with many of the issues we now confront.[22]

Chapter Four

INCONSISTENCIES
AND MISCALCULATIONS
OF THE MOVEMENT

It is well known that the movement is not without its
critics. I believe that the movement deserves better critics
—more consistent, more historically aware, less polemi-
cal, less defensive. Among its present critics are a
curious conglomeration of (1) right-wing political acti-
vists who are fighting "sex education in the schools,
fluoride in the water, and sensitivity training"; (2) some
psychotherapeutic professionals who see in encounter
groups the dangerous loss of control over professional
accreditation for therapeutic services; (3) Christian fun-
damentalists who are afraid of the trend toward the new
morality, sexual license, and touch therapy; (4) some of
the older generation of National Training Laboratories
leaders who fear fanaticism, eclecticism, and extrava-
gance in the ranks; (5) high school administrators
worried about teachers beginning to experiment with encounter groups in the public schools; and (6) certain
religious educators who are worried about the excesses
of anti-intellectualism in personal religious experiencing.[1]

One may have received the impression from earlier
chapters that our evaluation of the encounter culture is
so positive that the negative elements are virtually negli-

gible. If such an impression has been allowed to develop, it is now my task to correct it. The fact is that one of my principal reasons for writing at some detail on this subject is that I think the movement is more significant than do its critics, and in fact deserves wiser, more thoughtful criticism than it has received. To date the criticism of the movement has been little less fanatical than the movement itself.

A substantial part of our critical task has already been accomplished, or at least begun, in Chapter Two, where we have discussed the reasons why the movement has had difficulty thinking about itself historically. We will not in this chapter repeat our historical criticism of the movement, but focus rather on some philosophical and moral issues and on some of the practical abuses that are frequently encountered in the movement.

1. PHONINESS, BREVITY, AND ANTI-INTELLECTUALISM

a. Is the encounter culture really a "put-on"?

Why has a movement that has so emphasized honest self-disclosure and so opposed deception and dissimulation been criticized so often as being utterly phony and implausible? It is ironic that a movement which shouts so loud about "coming on straight" should be perceived by so many people as coming on with artificiality and sham in its procedures and perhaps in its very essence.

"The urge to fake it is almost irresistible," writes Ruitenbeek. "Most group members have been coached by friends and by promotional brochures; they believe that a peak experience is not only desirable but necessary, if one is to have fullest happiness and mental health. They are programmed for peaks. Further, elation or perceptual strangeness induced by mildly hypnotic or hallucinogenic techniques can easily provide the outward and visible signs of an inward awareness." [2]

Perhaps it is just because encounter groups idealize honesty so much that their less-than-honest practices appear so glaring. The insincere flaws of merchants of sincerity are not hard to recognize. They have a keen and constant eye for publicity. Few are poor. Fees are high. Some virtually live on faddism. The charisma of the leader may make or break him. The "success" of a group is not uncommonly judged by how many people have been "turned on," by the intensity of emotional response, or by the dramatic quality of interpersonal transactions. These practices do not lend credibility to exponents of absolute integrity.

b. Is the short-term format counter-productive to long-term intimacy?

Almost everyone in the movement would agree that he is searching for a deepening of the capacity for intimacy. Here lies one of my strongest objections. The intensive focus placed upon short-term interpersonal transactions (the encounter weekend, the microlab, the marathon, the intensive workshop) may be counter-productive in developing the kind of sustained long-term intimacy for which persons in our society so desperately hunger.

Has the movement relied too heavily upon the quicky, rootless relationship? Has it dealt deeply enough with facilitating growth in relationships of continuing long-term intimacy? Are not these the greater need of the "temporary society"?

The movement has made a great deal of its ability to achieve constructive change in a short time. Some of its claims are convincing. But this may actually exacerbate the tougher problem of how we are going to learn to live and share with others not just on the basis of an ecstatic weekend, but on the basis of continuing, long-term relationships of accountability, trust, and mutual care.

We suspect that one of the reasons for the short-term format of the encounter culture has nothing to do with its intentional design, but simply with the fact that these weekends and short-term slots are the only times available for the busy facilitators and consultants, many of whom hold full-time jobs that make it necessary for them to moonlight in order to do work with encounter groups. This is an understandable sociological reason for the short-term format, but that format has created its own genre of "reentry" problem." After one develops an intensive relationship with a group, it then becomes difficult to relate one's new understandings to the ordinary setting out of which one has come.

The movement has already received much stiff criticism, partially justified, for its inability to handle the reentry problem. There is sometimes a comic dimension in reentry, as we see in the movie *Bob and Carol and Ted and Alice*, with its awkward effort to transfer the intimacy of the group to broader relationships. Often the very degree to which the group process has been effective makes it increasingly difficult to achieve that transition.

The reentry problem is one with which the Christian tradition, and particularly Protestant pietism, has had considerable experience. The same question in frontier evangelical pietism focused on how to take a person who has had a conversion experience and nurture him as he moved back into his actual living environment so that he could express his new self-understanding amid the old "worldly" set of circumstances. That funded experience of Christian nurture might be immensely useful to the encounter culture. Its basic solution has been to provide the newly reborn with a continuing set of supportive resources, a continuing community of concerned persons with whom he will share learning, playing, worshiping, celebrating, confessing, and missionary involvement. Something analogous to that would be desirable for the encounter culture.

The religious community can make a significant contribution to group encounter in this respect, since it is already dealing with persons in continuing relationships. Here are persons whose lives are intertwined by repeated interactions, not merely persons on a one-shot encounter weekend. The prospect of engaging in intensive group encounter in the setting of religious institutions is much more promising than is ordinarily conceived.

c. Are encounter groups anti-intellectual?

Although it is unfair to categorize such a broad movement as anti-intellectual, I continue to be disturbed by an unchecked anti-cerebral *tendency* in the encounter culture which often damns the reflective process as contrary to experiencing, which views ideas only as means of hiding feelings, and which unwisely misconstrues Perls's injunction to "Lose your mind and come to your senses." However valuable it may be to focus on "here and now" experiencing, it is regrettable that this has come to mean for some a nasty polemic against critical reflection. I have seen eminent leaders of the encounter culture back away from critical dialogue in a seminar setting on the grounds that the criticisms made of their practices were all merely rooted in anger and able to be psychologized.

When all criticisms of the movement are dealt with as if they were based on the anger or anxiety of the critic, this results in a strange phenomenon—*the very movement that so emphasizes receiving feedback cannot itself receive feedback!* When the movement becomes so defensive that it already assumes *ipso facto* a lack of credibility among its critics, it hardly improves its own credibility as a movement that wants to come on straight.

When Perls says: "Lose your mind and come to your senses," [3] he means: Get into your awareness continuum and flow with your feelings, without rehearsing and intellectualizing your feeling flow in advance. But that sometimes becomes perverted by his followers into the idea that the rational faculty of man itself is inimical to self-fulfillment, to sensory experience, and to having pleasure.

The encounter culture has grown up largely apart from the educational establishment. Part of the reason for this unfortunate estrangement lies in the anti-cerebral polemics of the encounter culture. Encounter groups do not really want sustained critical dialogue on ideas. That all seems a waste of time. The university is concerned pre-eminently with the criticism of ideas. Ideas do not seem to interest many human potential leaders. They are interested more in strategies and techniques for achieving rapid behavioral change. So, regrettably, there does not seem to be much basis in the movement for developing a serious critical intellectual inquiry that could be rooted in the experiencing process. Thus the counter-productive tendency of the movement may be to separate mind and body, despite its disclaimers.

2. PERMISSIVENESS, PSYCHEDELICS, AND SENSATIONALISM

Before we turn to general philosophical and moral problems in group encounter, it is appropriate that we deal with several specific issues in encounter practice. The fact that the encounter culture does not seem to be able to police itself, or even to establish for itself standards that would prevent abuses of various sorts, is one of the more exasperating problems we face. Happily the abuses of which we speak are not characteristic of all groups, or perhaps of even the larger percentage of them. Nonetheless they are found frequently enough to deserve more explicit critical attention.

a. Is sexual permissiveness encouraged?

I am trying to address responsible criticism to the movement. As I raise the question of flippant or clandestine sexual involvement within the encounter context, I am not doing it out of spite or as a scare issue. Rather, I raise the question of sexuality within the framework of a deep appreciation of the new affirmation of the body that is occurring in the encounter context. This appreciation does not prevent us, but rather moves us to ask further: What are the boundaries of interpersonal eros in short-term groups? How and by whom and with what criteria are these boundaries to be drawn? The movement has not thought deeply enough about the limits and hazards of sexual experimentation.[4]

The movement creates a great deal of momentum toward physical touch, body contact, and intimate sharing, verbally and nonverbally, which in fact does encourage the kind of quasi intimacy that characterizes the short-term sexual involvement. There is little evidence upon which we can be reassured that the movement is willing to deal seriously with the complex dimensions of this issue.

The usual reply to this sort of concern is that everyone must take responsibility for his own behavior. That may be a cop-out. The injunction to take care of yourself is clearly inadequate for persons who do not know how to deal responsibly with themselves and others as sexual beings. There is in fact a persistent tendency in human sexuality to allow it to become obsessive. It is easily overwhelmed by sensationalism and seduced by the very kind of sensory momentum that takes place in the intensive group experience. The mere advice that everyone is responsible for his own bodily behavior may be formally correct, but it remains a disastrous simplism for those who have not matured psychologically and morally to the point where they are truly accountable as sexual partners.

When sexually charged, the short-term format is hardly capable of nurturing the kind of intimacy for which the movement is really hoping. The reputation that the growth centers have gotten as places where extraordinary sexual intimacies are permitted, and in fact where easy pick-ups are possible, is not an altogether undeserved reputation and has not just been concocted out of the critics' imagination.

Deeply engrained in the movement is the erotic mysticism of which D. H. Lawrence is still the best exemplar.[5] Accordingly, intensified erotic awareness, it is assumed, will deepen one's mystical participation in cosmic reality. If I can fully experience myself sensually as a body, I will share more fully in the mystery of the universe. The positive aspect of erotic mysticism is that it does in fact help us to return to the awareness that the sensorium is the gift of God capable of transporting man into ecstatic delight and inviting him into full sensory contact with the interpersonal environment.[6]

The particular problem of all human eroticism, however, is its tendency to become obsessive. Man is the leisure being for whom sexuality is a constant possibility. Unlike much animal sexuality, human sexuality is not limited by seasons of closeness and seasons of separation. Man has not learned well enough to enjoy his sexuality within the framework of social constraints, which are necessary and desirable in order for sexuality to become a greater means to a higher value, namely, intimacy, genuine interpersonal closeness, openness to the full presence of another human being. So, despite all talk about intimacy, I am not yet convinced that the encounter culture is that interested in actual, sustained intimacy, and I will not be convinced until it begins to perceive sexuality more profoundly as a means to intimacy and not as an end in itself.

b. Does the drug culture subtly influence the encounter culture?

It is unfortunately necessary for us to comment on the relation of the encounter culture to the drug culture. Most group facilitators specifically prohibit drug usage in encounter sessions and in general see the encounter culture as a constructive alternative to the drug culture. Yet it cannot be denied that some of the more influential leaders of the encounter culture have testified to the central importance of hallucinogenic drugs for their "religious" development.[7]

It is disturbing that so much of the encounter culture's talk of "religious experience" is so decisively shaped by the language, images, and ideology of the drug culture. Observe how the drug culture's language so easily translates itself into the encounter culture. With drugs, people "turn on." In encounter, people "turn on" to others and to themselves. The psychedelic drug experience with all its alleged color, beauty, intricacy, complexity, and flow of awareness easily becomes translated in the encounter culture to the quest for sensate experiencing, sensory awareness, the flow of the awareness continuum, etc.[8] Of course, the encounter turn-on is, in my judgment, a much healthier experience than the drug turn-on. But it is understandable that religious educators are suspicious of the fact that so much of the model for religious experiencing in the encounter culture has been transmuted directly from the drug culture with its constricted concept of "religious experience."

In discussing his own personal "religious quest," William Schutz writes: "The first memory I had of the change in my orientation as an atheistic scientist came on my first LSD experience. . . . I was vibrating with the cosmos. The feeling was one of ecstasy and orgasmic harmony. I was fully in tune with everything." [9] Schutz's colleague at Esalen, Bernard Gunther, after hearing Aldous Huxley lecture on the psychedelic drug experience, volunteered to be a subject in a research project with LSD being conducted by a Los Angeles doctor. Later Gunther reported: "Suddenly a whole new world of possibilities opened to me. I had shut myself off in muscular tightness. I felt a physical deadness and also a deadness of sensitivity and emotion. With LSD I realized that life was synonymous with flow and openness, feeling and sensation." [10] It was then that Gunther began to study mystical experience and to develop techniques in sensory awareness.

Those of us who have dealt with religious experience as a subject of professional study look upon this development with great ambivalence. On the one hand we welcome any serious and existentially motivated interest in religious experience, even if the initiating factors are questionable and dangerous. On the other hand, we can only feel jaundiced and reluctant about these developments in other respects. For a drug-induced "religious experience" remains a cheap trip and hardly more than a distorted mirror of authentic religious experience. Religious educators in touch with the encounter scene can only feel a sense of deep regret that this scene is not more deliberately in contact with the great and varied historic tradition of religious experiencing, and not more aware of some of its recurring fanatical temptations, which drug trips have intensified.

c. Is nudity idealized as a strategy for personal growth?

I do not intend here to discuss extensively, and thus to call further attention to, the nude groups, which I believe to be an infinitesimally small fraction of the encounter groups that are functioning today. The sensationalist aspect of these groups has unfortunately caused them to be publicized completely out of proportion.

At a minimal level of comment I would merely wish to agree with the mainstream of group facilitators in the movement who feel that nudity is no spectacular virtue. The experience of taking off one's clothes is hardly a reliable guarantee of the healing of human brokenness. The argument that nudity leads to honesty is just as spurious as the argument that native impulsivity is always preferable to social repression. The assumption that you can accept someone better with his clothes off than with his clothes on is certainly a constricted understanding of acceptance. No argument for group nudity is more absurd, however, than the overrated assumption that to remove inhibitions is to produce constructive growth.[11]

I can only add one criticism of the movement as a whole. The movement has tended to gather around itself a curious collection of trip-takers and experience-mongers. It seems happy with the aura of faddishness and with a P. T. Barnum type of sensationalism. Its own romantic consciousness has in fact encouraged these fauvist tendencies, and for that reason the movement is to be held accountable for its easy caricature as sensationalistic. It is not at all surprising that the communications media have picked out the nude groups as the one feature upon which to focus their publicity. My greater confidence, however, is in the actual mainstream of the movement, which views the nude groups as a passing phase, largely a creation of the media, which has little promise for the movement as a whole.

3. SOME PHILOSOPHICAL AND MORAL ISSUES

a. Are hidden ethical judgments absolutized?

It is a curious form of morality which insists that anything is permitted just as long as one is "in touch with his feelings." The Augustinian injunction, "Love God and do as you please" has been changed to, "Groove with your feelings and do as you please." We readily agree that being in touch with your experiencing process is valuable and growth producing. But when internal congruence becomes an absolutized ethic to which all other moral judgments are appealed, this is just as simplistic as the standard absolutized ethics that are so cheaply lambasted in the encounter culture. Surely other values impinge on human growth besides just "feeling one's feelings."

Commensurate with the overevaluation placed upon feelings is the consistent underevaluation placed upon moral commitment to societal structures. Does feeling my feelings help our society to achieve greater social justice? Perhaps it may, but to assume that it inevitably will is dangerous. The categorical imperative of the encounter culture is: "You *ought* to feel your feelings fully." The curious fact that this does not *sound* like a moral injunction does not make it any less so. Many alternative moral considerations, such as the value of privacy, of loyalty to one's social and marital commitments, of continuity in historical processes, may be overrun roughshod in the encounter situation in favor of the absolutist ethic of congruence.

It is understandable that Keen writes: "Some wonder aloud whether religiosity founded on peak experiences has any relation to moral commitments." [12] Rogers has given us a more plausible rationale than others for the view that increased congruence will produce more rather than less positive social and ethical behavior, but it is still a risk. It is an intellectual and sociological risk which has to be proven again with each new person in each encounter situation.

The single-minded emphasis on spontaneity is not the soundest basis upon which to build social models if the encounter culture intends those models to achieve durability and historical continuity. "Spontaneity is at the very core of psychic life, but it needs to be differentiated from untrammeled impulsivity. Only infants and very young children can afford such luxury." [13]

There are some persons whose feeling responses I would trust enough to engage with them in some risk-taking activity such as mountain-climbing or ocean-sailing, but there are others I know whose feeling responses I have seen enough of to be certain that I would not want to risk my life with them. Are not similar distinctions needed in group encounter? Should one in every case trust every person in every group at the same level of depth? Certainly not. But the encounter culture often uncritically assumes that all persons are finally trustable if only they fully feel their feelings.

Do positive behaviors inevitably result when a person gets in touch with his feelings? The widely shared assumption of the encounter culture is that if a person is able to experience fully what his body is saying to him, then he will be on the right track. Right track means he will do "good," presumably be a "better" person, more open, loving, capable of responsibility. All this rests upon an implausibly high estimation of the inherent moral capacity of man, and the belief that his immediate feeling process will lead him in an altruistic or at least a socially livable direction. It also rests upon an extremely low estimate of the tendency of man toward destructive aggressiveness, self-deception about his own thoughtlessness, and pride in his own competence.

So we question the moral frame of reference of much that lies at the center of the encounter culture. How can these inadequacies be corrected? Surely not by diminishing emphasis upon congruence. It is largely true that when persons get in touch with their feelings, positive behaviors result. But we are well advised not to forget that sometimes when persons get in touch with the actual range of their anger they commit murder. Sometimes when they get in touch with the real depths of their despair they commit suicide. Sometimes when a person comes into full awareness of his meaninglessness he becomes a psychopath or a drug addict. Not nearly enough attention has been given in the movement to the disciplining of the will or to the hazards of the undisciplined will.

b. Have we a new secular paganism?

We have seen emerge both within and alongside the encounter culture a strange new fascination with astrology, magic, and the occult. These deserve much more deliberate theological criticism than we are now prepared to give.[14]

The movement seems unperturbed by its own inconsistencies, however. For at the same time that it is affirming radical human freedom, it is toying with the view that man is fated under the stars, or locked into a chain of reincarnational recurrences.

Approvingly, William Schutz comments on astrology and tarot cards: "The idea that whatever is supposed to happen will happen greatly reduced my anxiety about the future on several occasions and even made some unpleasant events, like deaths, much easier to deal with." But what of their truth claims? Schutz answers: "The moon has a large influence on the tides, so why not on a person who is about two-thirds water. Hmm. A reading from the Tarot or from the astrological charts didn't seem markedly worse than a reading from psychological tests." [15] Sam Keen sums up the attitude of the soft revolution toward the occult when he says: "Many strange things may be true—E.S.P., astrology, magic,—so it is best to keep an open mind." [16]

The new secular paganism is a return to nature mysticism, primitive religious consciousness, and the worship of holy places. Eliade and Van der Leeuw [17] have prepared the ground for a more serious engagement with the primitive religious awareness, but the movement unfortunately seems bored by analytical works in the history of religions. It would rather do its own experimentation without the interference of historical research. At least it must be clear that Christian faith is neither nature mysticism nor a diffused pantheism. Although Christian faith in God the Creator celebrates the whole of creation as a gift worthy of full sensory engagement, God is not, finally, synonymous with nature. To celebrate creation at its deepest level is to celebrate the giver of creation.

Christian celebration of the flesh is not merely an act of sensory masturbation or of trying to stimulate peak experiences after the fashion of Paul Bindrim's immersion of groups in multiple sensory stimulae. Bindrim's basic strategy is just as counter-productive to authentic peak experiencing as is multi-partner orgasm counter-productive to sexual intimacy.[18]

In its hungry eclecticism and quasi-imperialistic fervor, the encounter culture has been willing to embrace or at least to provide an umbrella for many questionable practices of the primitive religious consciousness that cannot mesh with its own basic philosophy of freedom. The movement is drawn toward the bizarre, the fanatical, and the occult. I believe that its central interest has much more to share with the Judeo-Christian center than it has shared, but its fascination with religions of fate and with occult oddities does not make that sharing any easier.

c. Is God reducible to human experience?

I cannot agree with Gordon Kaufman's fear that "theological reflection would suffer if thought were always forced to remain in direct contact with immediate experience."[19] Theological reflection surely would benefit by a firm and constant experiential rootage. But Kaufman rightly protests the tendency to reduce the object of Christian worship to subjective religious experience.

In pietism, as in Schleiermacher, and also in the encounter culture, statements about God are often finally reducible to statements about the religious consciousness.[20] God becomes merely a consequent, a derivative, a referent of the feeling of absolute dependence in religious experience. The larger weight of the Judeo-Christian tradition is quite clear that God is not reducible to religious experience, but prior to and beyond all human history and experience whatsoever. God is not dependent upon our feeling of absolute dependence upon him.

Elsewhere [21] I have discussed, and need not repeat here, an analysis of the following questions: Why cannot a humanistic philosophy take into consideration the special presupposition that makes theology a distinctive science? In what sense can authenticity be conceptualized as a formal "ontological possibility" but not actualized as a factual or "ontic possibility"? In what sense does Christian theology affirm a notion of "general revelation" without denying the uniqueness of the Christ event? In what sense is natural man's "knowledge of 'God'" finally man's knowledge of himself? Why is it that man, being who he is as self-assertive man, cannot escape the self-assertiveness that makes him think he can escape it? How does God's love encounter man as a power that embraces man precisely amid his fallenness and self-assertiveness? Why it is impossible for man to become fully aware of his fallenness if he himself is completely fallen? The viewpoint developed in answer to these questions in my previous books *Radical Obedience* (chs. 2 and 3), *Kerygma and Counseling* (ch. 1), and *Contemporary Theol-*

ogy and Psychotherapy (ch. 6) may be applied without difficulty to the encounter culture.

If we have in group processes a reliable understanding of full functioning and to some degree an actualization of it, why do we need the Christian kerygma? Does not our talk of a "once for all deed of God" remain a remnant of mythological thinking if we cannot reduce it as well to this-worldly language? With Bultmann, I agree that this is the crucial issue: Is it possible to have a "naturalistic Christianity" or a Christian understanding of being without Christ? [22]

Can full-functioning be achieved by groups without revelation? It is precisely the phrase "without revelation" that the Christological tradition from Colossians to Bonhoeffer calls into question. For that phrase presupposes that it is possible even to conceive of being without revelation. According to the Johannine and Pauline witnesses, nothing is possible, not even the first act of creation, without revelation. Thus, to speak of being without revelation is already to speak mythologically.

Can groups actualize the Christian life without Christ? In a certain sense, yes, in the particular sense that the Christian life, or life in Christ, is not alien to man but consonant with his created being and his deepest intention. "By faith man enters upon the life for which he was originally created." [23]

At a more profound level, however, the authenticity or full human functioning for which the encounter culture strives is never fully actualizable apart from Christ. Yet Christ is incognito in the empathetic process. Since authenticity is never fully actualized, it is never even adequately conceptualized, except in response to a relationship in which one understands himself to be loved with an infinite forgiving love and understood by one in whom mistrust is impossible. Such a relationship is achieved in group encounter only in a limited way.

Authentic life is therefore fully optable only when we are met by the infinite forgiving love of God which meets man and embraces him even amid his fallenness. This we see happening partially in the intensive group experience—persons accept persons precisely amid their inauthenticity and fallenness. In a sense my companion deals with me as if I were other than I am, for he refuses to value me amid my guilt and depression exclusively as I value myself. He values me to some extent as I am valued by the accepting reality in life itself. That which occurs implicitly in this transaction is made explicit in the Christian message of God's occurring love. Thus the act of embrace and acceptance that I receive from my companion is based not solely on the private sympathy or initiative of my companion, or else it would present itself to me as hollow and phony. Rather, it comes to me through him from the heart of reality itself. The source of that acceptance has made itself known in Jesus Christ, as the eucharistic community knows and celebrates.

d. Is the movement introverted?

Despite its ideology of universal love and inclusivism, the encounter culture has an irritating tendency to underscore and polarize the differences between "insiders" and "outsiders." This can lead to the same sort of unconvincing self-righteousness of which the pietistic movement has often been justly accused. Pietism emphasized the purist elements of the converted community so strongly that it soon began to draw hard and fast lines between "saved" and "unsaved," godly and ungodly, and consequently lost its credibility. Just as in pietism, where there was a tendency to be overly critical of all established practices, whatever they were, and to consider the converted community as the bearer of salvation for the world, which apart from that community would be going to hell, so there are very similar attitudes to be found in encounter groups. Just as there was a difficult problem of in-group/out-group estrangement which required careful renegotiation in pietism when one spouse was "converted" or "got religion" without the other spouse, likewise in the encounter culture the renegotiation is equally difficult and has the same hazards and blocks.

e. Does the movement romanticize and exaggerate its own destiny and importance?

Like most movements that call for drastic change, this one does indeed romanticize and exaggerate.[24] Unfortunately the credibility of the movement is diminished when it solemnly entertains a quixotic image of its own role in human evolution. The movement sometimes reeks with a self-appointed messianism which imagines that whatever it is doing self-evidently is the wave of the future.

Rather than merely be amused at the comedy of this exaggeration, I prefer to see it in the context of a long Western (in almost no sense Eastern) tradition of romantic messianism, traceable through Joachim of Fiore, the medieval "free spirits," the egalitarian millenarians, the Taborites, Thomas Müntzer, the left wing of the Reformation, the Levellers, Tolstoy, the Oneida community, and many other social experimentalists.[25]

The other side of the coin of overseriousness about one's future is a lack of seriousness about one's past. One might think that a movement so dedicated to improving awareness might consider improving its own awareness of its own history. In the long run its messianic romanticism will probably have to be judged under the dictum that those who fail to study history are condemned to repeat it. The problem is that each time history's mistakes are repeated, the price goes up.

It is not surprising, therefore, that the movement should lack realism about the human predicament and the human limitation. It is less culpable in its operational practice than in its theoretical orientation. Operationally there is a probing concern to grasp the dynamics of human estrangement. At the ideological level, however, there is a persistent refusal by the movement to allow its clients to entertain the awareness that man might have intransigent limitations as an evoluting being; that man might really be "prone to sin and that continually"; that man might have a flawed will which will not be overcome through technology or new social inventions; that what is yet to come in world history might be even more horrifying than the past which they so self-righteously decry and are so happy we have "transcended"; that human misery is as much a part of human growth as joy and ecstasy; and that suffering may have a decisive role to play in the continuing evolution of man.

Chapter Five

ENCOUNTER
AND CELEBRATION

Thus far attention has been drawn chiefly to the historic roots of the encounter culture and its implicit theological assumptions. I have dealt more with ideas and interpretations than with practical change. This chapter shifts direction to ask in a practical sense whether it is possible for the movement to mesh with institutional religion. Can the encounter culture risk meaningful dialogue with established religious structures and with developing programs in Christian education and worship? What specifically do religious groups have to learn from encounter groups? And what do encounter groups have to learn from actual and existing religious communities? [1]

Although the effort will be brief and incomplete, I will attempt to show some general lines along which this dialogue can be implemented. In this connection four issues will be pursued: (1) Can we set forth some guidelines for new directions and potential hazards in transverbal experimentation in worship? (2) Can we learn again to use body language in liturgical expression? (3) Can we anticipate the stickiest issues with which religious institutions will have to grapple as they explore this explosive dialogue with encounter eclecticism? (4) How is the potential dialogue with the encounter culture relevant to the question of how religious institutions are going to deal or fail to deal with the emerging generation? All these questions rotate around the pivotal question of how dialogue can be implemented between existing religious communities and the encounter culture, not merely at the theoretical level, but in terms of the practical reshaping of the religious institutions and their secularized offspring.

1. GUIDELINES AND HAZARDS
FOR TRANSVERBAL EXPERIMENTATION
IN WORSHIP

The communications revolution has reshaped and resensitized our sensory apparatus. Traditional modes of worship, which are almost exclusively locked into verbal communication (the rhetoric of preaching, the reading of Scripture, the reciting of invocations, petitions, words of assurance, etc.), remain implausible to individuals whose senses have been shaped by electronic media. When we gather people together, set them row on row in pews, and address them with our sequences of linear reasoning consisting of words lined end on end, we are working against the stream of very powerful preconditioning patterns that influence them to turn us off before we have begun, since they have been bombarded for years by rapid-fire audio-visual images. They are accustomed to an involving form of communication created in part by the power of electronic media (McLuhan).

We put our congregations in a very awkward and unnatural box when we bring them into a huge room with pews in straight rows, destining them to a passive, listening role.[2] By the very process of distancing and space utilization, before a word has been said, we lock them into an authority/subordinate relationship that most modern men, and especially young people, find unconvincing. Our predisposition, of course, comes from a venerated tradition in which we understand ourselves to be standing under the authority of Scripture. But that authority is today searching for some means of expressing itself in terms of new social models involving more democratic understandings of choice.[3] The pews themselves make a clear nonverbal statement about what is going on that already presets all the patterns of social interaction which, with imagination, could be quite different.

One simple procedure that could reshape radically the community at worship would be to take out the pews and make the worship space more functional for a different set of interpersonal transactions. This of course has ancient precedence in Romanesque and Gothic cathedrals, where people stood to share in the celebration of the Mass without spatial roles being defined by seating. Pews are not made for dialogue. Judging by the appalled reaction I have received in response to this suggestion, I am convinced that the pews also give persons a sense of safety in distance which they find very difficult to give up, even if it is counter-productive to the kind of fellowship they hope to achieve.

We have so limited ourselves to verbal transactions in worship that it often seems wholly out of bounds to meet other communicants nonverbally: to touch, to embrace warmly, to experience many of the interpersonally involving liturgical acts which have been so important in the history of Christian celebration (such as the laying on of hands, the passing of the peace, the bathing of feet, the pageantry of feast days, etc.).[4]

We have limited ourselves largely to outmoded, Victorian body transactions: Handshakes are O.K.; arms around shoulders are not. A gentle nod of recognition is O.K.; a warm embrace, unthinkable. A touch on the other person's shoulder might be O.K. in some circumstances, but do not invade another person's body space unless it is absolutely necessary. A brief glance into another's eyes is all right, but do not behold another person with a warm, sustained, open, joyful gaze. With Victorian body models setting all the boundaries, the church is not a place for intimacy. It is a place only for formalized transactions.[5] So people feel cheated. But, the history of Christian worship abounds with nonverbal embraces, and with body language that facilitates koinonia. We have abundant historic precedent for transverbal experimentation in worship, but it is a difficult step for us to take, because we are hooked on thinking about worship finally as a linguistic event.

How do we learn to touch, to be embraced by another as a celebration of God's drawing near? How do we begin in the context of the church to feel nonverbally the strength of others, or to experience being supported by them? Can we learn to trust by bodily entrusting ourselves into someone else's hands? All these issues are being explored in encounter group processes.

I would like to belong to a local church where a group of people were committed to asking what it means for us to act out our Christian community nonverbally. How can we embody trust and forgiveness in something more than just words? This demands a new type of liturgical experimentation. If this can occur in meaningful interaction with the Christian tradition, and in the light of the revision of modern man's sensory ratios, then it will be possible to praise God in the interpersonal idiom of the late twentieth century.[6] Without experimentation we can continue marginally to serve those over thirty-five, and those over sixty fairly well, but that will last only a few years. We must inevitably deal with an emerging generation nurtured on a different scale of sensory ratios, a generation wholly unconvinced by our wordy non-acts of worship.

Since our congregations span the generation gap, however, we have the more difficult task of developing dual competencies that reach out for both the very old and the very young. We must root ourselves in the deeper intentions of traditional preaching and worship, and at the same time experiment boldly with a new celebrative life-style that is now only in the process of being formed.

But why is this discussion on liturgy included in a book about the encounter culture? Because I am convinced that the human potential movement has many resources that would be useful in worship's experimental thrust. The experimenting church has good reason to be more deliberately in dialogue with the National Training Laboratories, with the Esalen network, and with the many others who are experimenting with the intensive group process, the expansion of human awareness, meditation, nonverbal communication, and the rediscovery of intimacy.

Can we anticipate some hazards in nonverbal liturgical experimentation? Just as in the encounter culture, so in liturgical experimentation our efforts may easily degenerate into an endless search for novelty. Our experimentation may become excessively preoccupied with the media of communication, with technological gimmickery, or with group processes per se, so that the means become confused with the end.

In its quest for relevance, liturgical experimentation sometimes fails at the most crucial point to announce the kerygma, the proclamation that Jesus is the Christ. If the name Jesus Christ is not heard, there is no Christian worship, since that name points to an event that cannot be fully grasped without encountering the person Jesus of Nazareth, in the presence of whom our talk of God takes on infinitely greater concreteness and clarity.

The danger of subjectivism lurks in all our efforts when we value the act of worship only in terms of how we feel about it, rather than of the divine reality to which worship is a response. The center of worship then becomes the worshiper and not the giver of life before whom the worshiping community finally stands. However elementary, let us remember that prayer is addressed to God and not to the neighbor. It is a transpersonal, never merely an interpersonal, act. Corporate worship is dialogue with God in the presence of the neighbor. Although we commend the experimental attitude, it often tempts us to frame issues on the purely horizontal level of interpersonal transactions, instead of on the level of the dialogue of man with God that is present and hidden within our dialogue with each other.

Another hazard is divisiveness, or the tendency to fragment the Christian community unnecessarily. When persons have long associated certain gestures, actions, and words with worship, and with long sentimental accumulations, anyone who innovates will come under attack. We must try hard, in our experimentation, to show these people that we are thinking out of a sense of historic continuity with the same tradition that they revere. Innovation risks dividing the body of Christ, filling it with pride and defensiveness on both sides of each issue. We are wise to try to embrace in our liturgical experiments those who oppose experimentation in an effort to hold on to their own roots. Thus pastors are ill-advised to initiate changes in worship unilaterally, but rather should work through worship committees or study groups who have been responsibly assigned the task of trying to think through what it means to be a celebrating community in the twentieth century.

2. BODY LANGUAGE IN LITURGICAL INNOVATION

What follows is an experiment in transverbal communication that may be appropriately done in a large sanctuary or a worship setting with ample space available. As persons arrive, they are ushered in according to a preset pattern. They are deliberately seated as far as possible from each other in the available space. The bigger the space the better. The first four participants to arrive are asked by ushers to sit in the four corners of the room. As others arrive they are ushered to points as far as possible from any other person. A call to worship, an invocation, a hymn, and Scripture may precede the following introduction.

WORSHIP LEADER: "Today we are asking you to be seated in an unusual way as a part of our service of worship, which is to be a body-language meditation. You are sitting at a distance from your nearest neighbor in order to reflect on what it means to be isolated or alienated from others. The Christian community exists as a community gathered to remember God's action in history, and to share in his love. But there are times when we do not feel that we are sharing in his community of love. We feel alone. This distancing experience is a way of nonverbally enacting that aloneness, with the hope that we can reinterpret it and transcend it.

"Close your eyes. Experience your separation. Risk feeling real distance from others. Intercede for the lonely, for those who are not in touch with others. Pray in your heart for prisoners; for the anxious and depressed; for those who live in their own imaginary world, and whose whole lives are separated from reality. Intercede for the elderly, separated from their families; for divorced persons, separated from those with whom they were once close; for children who feel lonely and lost; for all who experience radical loneliness. We pray each one for ourselves, also, in the silence of this room, asking that God the Spirit may enable each one of us to move toward greater closeness with others, toward the full embrace of those for whom we care, toward intimacy with those with whom we daily share our lives.

"When you have truly prayed for the lonely, open your eyes. Look around you. Visually behold your neighbors. As if seeing them for the first time after a long separation, behold with joy their faces, the look in their eyes. Visually survey the remarkable people in your midst. Turn around and behold each one. These are the ones, the Gospel suggests, through whom God intends our loneliness to be healed. Behold each one as God's gift to you. (*Pause.*)

"After you have truly beheld your neighbors, please stand up and imagine that your feet are bolted to the floor. You cannot move your feet. Now reach out for the nearest person. Try hard to touch him without moving your feet. Stretch. Try for another." (*If some are close enough to reach others, they will grasp hands. If they are so far distant that none can reach another hand, that is all the better. Let them experience the unfulfilled hunger for another's hand.*)

"Now, having reached out longingly for our neighbors, let us be seated and hear the word of Scripture: 'But now in Christ Jesus you who once were far off have been brought near in the blood of Christ. For he is our peace, who has made us both one, and has broken down the dividing wall of hostility . . . that he might create in himself one new man in place of the two, so making peace, and might reconcile us both to God in one body through the cross, thereby bringing the hostility to an end.' (Eph. 2:13–16.) The way in which God intends loneliness to be overcome has been made known in history, and above all in the Christ event. For God himself has sought fellowship with man. God has chosen to be with us—Emmanuel—in our midst, close to us, through the ministry of one man in history, and through men in history who trust and share his self-disclosure.

"Although there may indeed be times for solitude, in the broader stream of life we are called to be together, to bear one another's burdens, to share what we have to give to others. In such a powerful divine gift as sexuality, God brings persons close to each other. In fact, the sexual form of intimacy may be a prototype of other human forms of intimacy. For there, what is incomplete in one is made complete by the other. Indeed we may not always experience intimacy with sex, but sexuality remains a God-created drive that virtually impels us in the direction of closeness with another human being. It is an astonishing parable of man's being together, and of all human covenant partnership. Not only in sexuality does God draw us together, but also in the closeness and warmth of friendship, in the fellowship of shared tasks of moral and intellectual growth.

"You have been positioned, against your preference, so as to underscore the distance between persons. But the time for distance is over. In response to the Gospel, it is a time for searching for some means of moving toward closeness.

"As you look around and behold the others in your midst, think of one person from whom you may feel at a particular distance, with whom you would like to be nearer. In order to be more intentional, choose any-one except a person sitting nearest to you. Or select a person whom you believe needs your nearness or affirma-tion or pardon, or from whom you need nearness, affir-mation, or pardon. When I give a signal, you may stand up and begin to move toward that person. Come as near to him as you want. You may move halfway, or only one step, or all but one step, or completely into his presence with a handshake or an embrace. Choose a distance that feels right with that person. If someone else chooses you, respond to his movement in a way that feels right to you. You will end up in pairs. Now enact your movement toward your neighbor. Let this be nonverbal. Let your body say to your neighbor whatever seems most fitting. (*Pause.*) Now you have a few minutes to talk about what is happening inside you and within your partner. (*Pause.*)

"Having shared your feelings with your partner, you may look for two other persons in a pair whom you would like to incorporate into your circle. Move toward them as a reenactment of God's reconciling love. (*Pause.*) Now as you stand together in small groups, close your eyes and experience your particular group's being together. If there are things you want to say, do not say them, but try to communicate them without words. (*Pause.*) Now we ask all groups to come together near the altar. We will all stand in one circle, arm in arm. As we move together, let us experience ourselves as a unique community. What does it feel like to be this particular community, to share our lives with these particular human beings? (*Pause.*)

"We conclude this act of reconciliation with a prayer of gratitude for our life together. (*Here may be used extemporaneous prayers, or the following prayer*):

"O God our Father, you who have shared yourself with us are at work to break down barriers between us. You who have acted to forgive all sorts of human alienation and brokenness have set the course of history in a radical crisis by confronting us with your pardoning, merciful love. We thank you for this circle of persons, and for what each one now means to us, and for the simple presence of each person here. We are grateful to share in your being through the being of each one here. We are grateful that your love has made itself known through the presence of each person in this circle. We intercede for those in our community not in this circle, and especially for those who do not share intimately in any human community. We ask that you would awaken us to what it means to embrace them and to draw them into the circle of fellowship with you. Enable us through the power of your love to share your love with the world at hand, the same love that is made known to us in Jesus of Nazareth, in whose spirit we pray. Amen."

3. THE DEMAND FOR RISK-TAKING

What follows is an imaginary conversation among the board members of a local church considering experimentation in group encounter.

CHAIRMAN: O.K. Let's call this board meeting of the Ridgedale Community Church to order. Pastor, I believe you are the first on the agenda . . . with a proposal on . . . let's see . . . What? Encounter groups?

PASTOR: Yes, thank you. The proposal I am making has already been discussed and approved by the church's committee on education. We would like to ask your advice and consent in the development of a new program in experimental education for adults, especially young adults, for twelve Friday evenings this spring. These sessions would focus on intensive group encounter, seeking to develop clearer communication among people in our congregation. Some of our sessions would experiment with nonverbal communication, using role reversals, simulation learning, and Gestalt techniques to get us more into our feelings and more aware of what others are feeling. By means of encounter group processes, we hope to discover in a fresh way something about what it means to be a Christian community.

FINANCE CHAIRMAN: Is this what you studied when you went to the Sun Valley Retreat Center for several days last month?

PASTOR: Yes, I was serving as a group facilitator there. I have participated in a variety of laboratory-learning experiences over the last few years. Several of these have been important to me personally, but only recently have

I begun to think about what a difference they might make for us as a church, and how these group processes might help us develop a deeper sense of community.

EDUCATION CHAIRMAN: Some of us who are involved in the educational work of this church have come to feel that the time has arrived to risk some new departures, even if it means experimenting in directions where we cannot control all the consequences. Our educational program is not making spectacular headway these days. If this program would enrich our being together as an intimate human family in the way that the early church apparently experienced itself, then I think it is a risk worth taking.

BOARD MEMBER: What does it have to do with the Bible, Pastor?

PASTOR: The Bible helps us to understand the extent of our estrangement from each other and before God. In growth groups of this sort we learn very quickly about our own alienation from each other. The Bible witnesses to God's forgiving love and accepting grace, which frees us to trust each other more fully. In groups of this sort I have seen people experience deep acceptance through other persons in a way that is a great deal like God's acceptance of us. The Bible presents us with a pattern of the good life and teaches us what it means to love one another and care for one another as God loves and cares for us, and to be in an open and trusting relation with one another. Effective encounter groups help those types of behavior to be achieved.

CONSERVATIVE MEMBER: Wait a minute. Are you talking about "sensitivity training"? From what I have heard, that is part of an ultraliberal attempt to break down the traditional standards of morality in this country. I have heard they use brainwashing techniques and propagate the new morality. They encourage sexual intimacies and emphasize people touching each other. Frankly, Pastor, I doubt that sensitivity training has anything to do with the church's work, and if these reports are true, it may be the worst enemy of the church.

EDUCATIONAL CHAIRMAN: Gentlemen, I have talked at some length with the education committee, and I must say I am enthusiastic about this proposal. Our educational efforts are pretty thin right now, and if our critics know a way to improve them, we would like to hear their constructive suggestions.

We want our educational process to be something more than just an act of rote learning or a ritualized pastime. But how do we get people beyond formalities? How do we break through to where persons are genuinely in touch with each other's feelings? That is what many persons in our church are seeking these days, hoping the church will have an answer for them.

Obviously they are finding this in encounter groups outside the church. Are we going to offer them canned ideas about religion, or a live process of religious experiencing? It is not a good enough answer to say that the church cannot reach them at this deeper level. In the church's history, it has for centuries been involved in building communities that have reached down into persons' real needs.

CONSERVATIVE MEMBER: Now wait a minute. You have not answered my question about these sensitivity training groups being left-wing inspired or part of a radical liberal conspiracy. This is not just my idea. A lot of people think this. I have never attended one of these groups, and I do not intend to do so, but in my opinion and from what I've heard they are dangerous and the church should keep its hands off. It would be very controversial.

PASTOR: But surely it is not the church's task simply to avoid controversy. If pure tranquillity had been the church's mission, it would never have proclaimed the gospel. As to the charge that this is a left-wing, new morality movement contrary to the Christian tradition, I have shared in many different encounter groups and frankly I have never heard anyone express anything that sounded to me like Communist propaganda. I see little in common between Marxist ideology and personal-growth groups. In fact, Communist societies would more likely be terribly afraid of letting encounter groups take shape within their society because the whole process of group encounter involves a free self-expression of who one is.

CONSERVATIVE MEMBER: Yes, but what about the nude groups?

PASTOR: A great deal of wild publicity has been given to so-called nude encounter groups. Among all the groups in which I have participated, never have I met a person who had even been in a nude group, and never have I met a leader who thought that nudity was advisable. Of the thousands of encounter groups that are being conducted each year, I would judge that only a fraction of 1 percent of them are the nude groups that get so much publicity. Naturally, when tabloid magazines hear of such a group, they write their exposé. But please do not conclude that nudity is a usual thing with encounter groups or that it has anything particularly to do with what we are proposing.

CONSERVATIVE MEMBER: But don't you think encounter

groups are exponents of the new morality and of freer sexual ethics?

PASTOR: Encounter groups take people as they are, and they would take church people as they are as sexual beings and deal with their feelings as they exist at the present moment. This would involve people trying to understand themselves in new ways as persons who hunger for intimacy with others. But I don't perceive the encounter group as being an exponent of a particular dangerous moral philosophy. It is simply a means for providing a clear feedback to you on how you come across to me at the present moment.

CONSERVATIVE MEMBER: How do I come across to you at the present moment?

PASTOR: Well, I am experiencing you now as needing to protect something that is very valuable to you, namely, the order and decency that you associate with traditional Christian worship and Christian education.

CONSERVATIVE MEMBER: Well, that is the way I feel. I think I have something good to defend and I would like to see you try to defend it too.

PASTOR: I too am committed to order and decency, but I am also committed to depth and significance in Christian worship and education. I am not sure, however, that the present design of worship and education is fully adequate to achieve those goals and I would like to see us experiment wisely. After all, the church has been experimenting with worship and education for the entire twenty centuries of its existence, so this is nothing new. The church is constantly being called upon to respond to new historical situations with its own understanding of history, and that is what I would hope to see happen now.

EXPERIENCED ENCOUNTER GROUP PARTICIPANT: I would like to speak up here and say that a lot of these criticisms are nonsense. I have been involved the last several months in a growth center, trying to discover what is being done there, trying to discover myself and how I can benefit from the center's learnings. It has helped me a great deal to get in touch with my feelings, to listen to others, and to hear what others feel about me. In fact, after I come back from the growth center experience, I feel terribly alienated in the service of worship and in the church's educational settings, because they are so formal and pretentious. People do not listen to each other. They are not interested in really getting in contact with each other. It is all so dull.

CHAIRMAN: What do you think we could do in the church to serve those who have been involved in encounter groups who would like to see something similar happen in the church in order to relate that type of experience to their Christian experience?

PASTOR: This is exactly what our proposal hopes to do. We want to develop a series of evening sessions to which persons, largely adults or young adults, could come, share their feelings, and, in effect, function as an encounter group. We hope they would also find within the framework of Christian love a community of people who are specially concerned to understand themselves as Christians in the midst of this experience, and, let's say, to share the love of God through human love. Now what is so threatening about that?

CONSERVATIVE MEMBER: I am certainly not threatened by sharing the love of God, but I do wonder what will happen to preaching in the midst of all of this frantic search for encounter. The Bible speaks with authority and the purpose of preaching is to express the Biblical witness to us in clear terms.

PASTOR: The learning process that goes on in encounter groups can be supportive of authentic Biblical preaching, in my opinion, because human needs will be better defined. I would like to try to show through preaching, how the Biblical witness speaks to human needs as they are expressed in the intensive group experience.

CONSERVATIVE MEMBER: Pastor, I can't help seeing this as an enormous risk and diversion. It is risky because all sorts of people may get involved in this project with whom we do not agree around here. All sorts of persons may do all kinds of things, even in the church—you know, like hugging—that just do not belong in the church. I see it as a diversion because it diverts us from our true purpose which is to proclaim the Biblical message and to convert people to Christian experience.

EDUCATION CHAIRMAN: I certainly admit the risk factor, but, frankly, I am willing to take the risk. It seems to me that our own more cautious alternatives are not really meeting our parishioners where they actually are.

PASTOR: I think it is a risk, too, but let me speak to the point about it being a diversion. I think it can seriously be argued that what is happening in encounter groups today is very much in tune with the history of Christianity and especially with the tradition of pietism out of which we have come. Most of our history has been strongly shaped by the movements of eighteenth- and nineteenth-century Protestantism which strongly emphasized small groups caring for each other, confessing their sins, proclaiming the Word, and being supportive of one another in an intensive group context. So I view the encounter group as standing in a profound, hidden continuity with our own history.

CONSERVATIVE MEMBER: Pastor, you seem to be rather uncritically embracing the whole encounter movement as something that can be directly taken over by the church. I am just wondering if you have any serious criticisms of it. Why does it have such a bad reputation? Why are so many people so defensive and so wary of sensitivity training? And why does it seem to us like something so alien to the church's life?

PASTOR: The question is well taken. I do in fact have some serious criticisms of groups in which I have participated. Despite my basically positive evaluation, I nonetheless feel that encounter groups have some serious limitations. In some of the groups I have been in, for example, the leaders are manipulative. Some groups are coercive, and get people into situations where they are under pressure to reveal themselves. Another objection I have to some groups is their tendency toward faddism, picking up new things to do, with novelty as an end in itself. The process can become superficial and repetitive. This is something we would try to avoid. Also there is a kind of romanticism and naïveté about the human predicament in the encounter culture. Some people imagine that if we could just get everybody into encounter groups, we could solve the world's problems, and that all human dilemmas, from warts to international diplomacy, are reducible to simple problems of emotional blockage or of interpersonal communication. I have also been in groups in which I felt that the kinds of intimacy that men and women were developing had spin-offs in sexual involvements that I did not regard as healthy. So I am not without my own criticisms of these groups, but taken as a whole, their direction is of positive value and the objections that I have raised are objections to the inadequate functioning of particular groups, and not to the intended nature of the group encounter itself. They were just bad encounter groups and I would hope that whatever is done within the framework of the Christian community would avoid those particular aspects. As a matter of fact, I think that the Christian ethic helps us to solve some of the problems that are prevalent in the so-called secular encounter group.

SUPPORTIVE MEMBER: You have convinced me that we need to experiment some in this area, although I think we should be rather cautious. What would you suggest we do?

PASTOR: Well, as I suggested earlier, I think that the first thing would be an evening encounter series using either my own resources as a facilitator or those of some other available person who has been involved in group leadership. The seminaries are beginning to train men in this area and perhaps a young seminarian might be available to take over some of these responsibilities in our religious education department. I would also like to see us experiment with worship to try to discover some new forms of relating to each other nonverbally in the acts of confession, thanksgiving, and self-offering. In other words, I think the processes of Christian education and Christian worship stand to benefit a great deal from the learnings that are being achieved in the behavioral sciences in their studies of human encounter.

CONSERVATIVE MEMBER: I would like to raise one more serious question about all of this. I have visions of people cracking up, blowing their stacks, having psychotic breaks, and causing all kinds of crazy things to happen. In groups like this don't you really need a trained clinical psychologist to do this work for you? I mean surely you wouldn't get involved in something like group therapy and pawn that off as Christian education, or reduce Christian education to group therapy, or pretend that you have credentials as a therapist, would you?

PASTOR: I am glad you raised the question, because it is important to make a distinction between therapy and education. Therapy, which is basically intended for people who are ill, must be done by psychiatrists or psychologists. It is important to make a distinction between therapy and intensive group experiencing which is aimed at improved communication among basically normal people. I consider myself a pastor, not a therapist. I do not have any desire to engage in therapy, and certainly do not claim to do therapy. My only desire is to help persons to discover who they are and to grow by learning to communicate more clearly with each other. I would make it clear to all persons entering our group that they should not think of it as a place where they can expect psychotherapy. Rather, I would prefer that they think of it as a place where they can get clear feedback from other persons concerning their behavior to feelings. As a matter of fact, a study of groups by Jack Gibb has shown that in many cases leaderless groups are more effective than groups with authoritarian leadership or professional leadership of any kind. So when I speak of myself as a facilitator of group communication in this group I do not mean that I would be taking a strong leadership role, in an authoritarian sense. I would only be trying to help persons in the group to communicate clearly with each other.

UNCONVINCED MEMBER: But what would be your subject of study? Are you going to study the Bible? Or are you going to study psychology? Or are you going to study Christian ethics? Are you going to read books? What do you want to study?

PASTOR: The subject of study in the intensive group experience is one's self and one's relationships with others. It is as if one's self were the book that we are reading and the interpersonal relationships that are now taking place the subject matter at hand. We are trying to read that "book" accurately. In order to read that "book" we may have to read other books, and there are many available. A bibliography will be provided for persons who want to do further reading. But the essential subject matter is our here and now experiencing. I think that has something important to do with the study of the Biblical witness. For through group encounter we may move toward the quality of Christian fellowship to which the New Testament calls us in Jesus Christ.

SUPPORTIVE MEMBER: Mr. Chairman, in the light of all that has been said, I would like to move that our church engage in a new experiment in group encounter which would be led by the pastor and would follow along the lines he has described.

A motion has been made that the church initiate a program of encounter groups for adults hoping to achieve a level of trust, intimacy, and community which could be understood as an expression of God's love and care. How would you vote on this motion? What are some questions you would raise in addition to the ones that were raised? How well were the objections answered? Does this appear to be a promising direction, or does it have pitfalls that have not been recognized? How can the learnings that are being achieved in encounter settings be utilized by the Christian community? These are among the issues with which I have been wrestling in this book. Admittedly my entire argument has an introductory character and much more work lies ahead. My immediate purpose will be fulfilled, however, if these issues have been framed in a clear enough fashion that they can be more resolutely pursued by responsible religious groups within the limits of their specific settings.

4. YOUTH CULTURE AND ENCOUNTER CULTURE

The encounter group is an intergenerational equalizer. What is happening in youth culture is also happening in the encounter culture—honest self-disclosure, the breaking of facades, getting in touch with oneself and others, the recovery of primary community, the struggle against depersonalization, erotic mysticism, the new hunger for transpersonal religious experience, the resensitizing of awareness.[7] Much is to be shared between youth culture and the encounter culture.[8]

Most theological works are unconsciously addressed to the older or controlling generation. I hope this discussion will find its way into the hands of the emerging generation. It is evident that perplexed churchmen have been struggling for some time to make Christian community more credible to the emerging generation without losing touch with the historic Christian tradition or the adult generation which is trying to mediate it. That is part of the reason I have found myself fascinated by the style of communication of encounter groups. Even though the clientele is largely over thirty, they nonetheless share in a life-style that is native to youth culture.[9]

Broad experimentation is going on in our society concerning what it means to share in a human community in intimacy, warmth, and mutual support. A new human product is being molded. In communities of experimentation, the new man and the new society are being shaped in their embryonic forms. In communes and encounter groups, persons are learning to experience themselves as socially accountable. They are experimenting with models of societies in which they conceivably might wish to live. There is an implicit social model-building function going on both in the encounter culture and in the youth culture. In a society that is urgently hungering for new social models, this experimentation takes on exceptional significance.

The emerging generation is correct to demand and hope for richer sensate experiencing than that which has been bequeathed them by their fathers' generation. They know they must become more at home as bodies than their fathers ever were or could be. When we speak of the demand for a deeper sexuality, however, we are not speaking of genital sexuality only, but of fully embracing our bodily and erotic existence. Too often we limit sexuality to genital sexuality. The sexual revolution is pressing for more general sensate discovery, the eros of sight and taste, the full range of body experiencing, the joy of touch, the total employment of sensory faculties. In this respect both youth culture and the encounter culture are turning the same corner. Even if this hunger may be offensive to the parent generation, it must be fed. God's gift and demand in our time is that we receive and fully accept our bodily existence.[10]

I say to the emerging culture: What you are doing is not as distant from the Christian tradition as you might have imagined. Even your more radical experimentation has precedents within the Judeo-Christian tradition that deserve your attention. You are not best served by historical unawareness or ignorance. The quest for intimacy is not new to this generation. Other generations have hungered for peace, searched for new social models, dreamed utopian dreams. Your hunger for sensory awareness is anticipated by Augustine and Francis of Assisi. You have deep roots in the mystic tradition, with your awareness of the ability of small things to freight vast meanings, and your desire to sensitize the spirit to the subtly changing shapes of life.

Youth culture is not rebelling today against the heart of their Western religious traditions so much as against distortions of them. Youth seem to have given up in disgust on the renewal of institutional Christianity, but that disgust itself stands in a profound tradition of Christian ecclesiology.[11] They have less quarrel with the center of the Christian message than with what they actually behold in the Christian communities they have met. There is little difficulty in showing the kinship between the values of the encounter culture and many historic Christian values.[12] What is more difficult to show is how the encounter culture might relate meaningfully to actual and existing Christian communities.

One of the most fundamental challenges that youth culture makes to the church is: We do not want to hear you talk about love. We want to see it happen in communities of love. We do not want to hear your words about joy. We want to see joyful persons. We want none of your talk of forgiveness. We want to see a community where forgiving, accepting love is happening and changing personal behavior.

With our idolatry of words, we are not prepared for the profundity of this statement. We are hardly prepared to respond to it with anything more than more useless words. Yet it is a decisive challenge.

Understandably we lose our credibility unless we nurture communities that embody the love, forgiveness, and reconciliation to which we so cheaply point with our words. We do not now need more words about love or community. We need a loving community. Theology can serve the Christian community today by helping to bridge the gap between the older word-oriented generation and the younger action-oriented generation, but not merely with more words. Theology must serve by helping to grasp the actual means of embodying in living communities the concepts we so easily discuss abstractly.

Bonhoeffer may be speaking directly to our situation when he says that there may be nothing that we can say for a while about Christian faith that will have credibility. Rather, it is necessary that we live out our faith nonverbally before God without "God." "The God who is with us," says Bonhoeffer, "is the God who forsakes us (Mark 15:34). The God who makes us live in this world without using him as a working hypothesis is the God before whom we are even standing." [13] Before God and with him we live without the "God" of classical theism. However uncomfortable, this is where we are today in Christian theology. We are trying to find out what it means to live out the Christian life without the verbal crutches. Again Bonhoeffer is our guide, writing from prison that we are being "driven back to first principles. . . . During these years the Church has fought for self-preservation as though it were an end in itself, and has thereby lost its chance to speak a word of reconciliation to mankind and the world at large. So our traditional language must perforce become powerless and remain silent, and our Christianity to-day will be confined to praying for and doing right by our fellow man. Christian thinking, speaking and organization must be reborn out of this praying and this action." [14]

The transverbal act is thus being demanded of us at the very time the verbal crutch is being denied us. Our God-language is being taken away from us. That does not mean that God is taken away from us. We in our century have experienced the death of traditional, theistic God-language, not the death of God. God-language is not dead for everyone, but for many in the modern world it has lost its power and plausibility.

Obviously those committed to the continuity of their religious tradition must not only know God-language in its historical phases but also how to translate its intent into contemporary language. We must know what the Christian tradition has meant when it speaks of God acting in history, of salvation, of God's reign, etc. But we may have been deprived of the opportunity of using that language effectively in the contemporary context where many (although not all) are unprepared to hear it. So our tougher task becomes learning how to *embody* personally and interpersonally those meanings to which the Christian tradition has pointed with God-language. This embodiment may be done with the aid of language, but finally it must show forth in human actions and not merely in words.

Our most recent disease in Protestant theology has been called hermeneutics. Admittedly certain growth took place during the period of that disease.[15] But the irony of the hermeneutic episode was that despite detailed talk of the "word-event," it was unable to translate its words into events. Despite much talk of clear communication, it actually communicated with esoteric vagueness. Despite its pretenses about being a general movement in the service of the church's proclamation, it actually functioned as a very small "in" crowd which wrote mostly to each other. There was something in the movement which decisively denied itself, viz., its unwillingness to risk the very event-theology it proclaimed. It remained content to view the theological task essentially as one of words. That is a radical fault. If you cannot do what you say is at the heart of what you say must be done, you commit not a peripheral but a central error.

I am proposing that the intensive group process can be, when proper boundaries are defined and critical qualifications made, a creative milieu for spiritual growth and a lively context for religious discovery, and thus, for theological inquiry. The intensive group experience can be a locus of rethinking the tragedy of man's alienation from himself and others, and in a deeper sense from the giver and ground of life. It can be a context for reexamining man's covenant with God by means of concretely reestablishing and redefining our human covenants with our neighbors. It can be a vital context for probing the meaning of the love of God through the rediscovery of the love of others, even though infinite divine forgiving love is never finally reducible to human love. The intensive group experience can be a context for putting these things together, for searching for the whole equation, and for integrating one's personal history.

Notes

Introduction: THE ENCOUNTER CULTURE

1. Frederick S. Perls, *Gestalt Therapy Verbatim* (Real People Press, 1969); Frederick S. Perls and others, *Gestalt Therapy* (Julian Messner, Inc., 1951); Frederick S. Perls, *Ego, Hunger and Aggression* (George Allen & Unwin, Ltd., 1947); Joen Fagan and I. L. Shepherd (eds.), *Gestalt Therapy Now* (Science and Behavior Books, 1970).

2. Alexander Lowen, "Bio-energetic Group Therapy," in Hendrik M. Ruitenbeek (ed.), *Group Therapy Today* (Atherton Press, Inc., 1969).

3. Warren G. Bennis, Edgar H. Schein, Fred I. Steele, David E. Berlew (eds.), *Interpersonal Dynamics: Essays and Readings on Human Interaction*, rev. ed. (The Dorsey Press, 1968); Richard L. Batchelder and J. M. Hardy, *Using Sensitivity Training and the Training Laboratory Method* (Association Press, 1968).

4. Jacob L. Moreno, *Who Shall Survive?* rev. and enlarged (Beacon House, Inc., 1953).

5. For a general introduction, see Jane Howard, *Please Touch: A Guided Tour of the Human Potential Movement* (McGraw-Hill Book Co., Inc., 1970); Rasa Gustaitis, *Turning On* (The New American Library, Inc., 1969); Stuart Miller, *Hot Spring: The True Adventures of the First New York Jewish Literary Intellectual in the Human-Potential Movement* (The Viking Press, 1971); Hendrik M. Ruiten-

beek, *The New Group Therapies* (Avon Books, 1970).

6. For an introduction to small-group research, see Alexander Paul Hare, *Handbook of Small Group Research* (The Free Press of Glencoe, Inc., 1962); Dorothy Stock, "A Survey of Research on T groups," in Leland Powers Bradford and others (eds.), *T-Group Theory and Laboratory Method* (John Wiley & Sons, Inc., 1964); R. F. Bales, "A Set of Categories for the Analysis of Small Group Interaction," *American Sociological Review*, Vol. XV (1950), pp. 257–263; Wilfred R. Bion, *Experiences in Groups* (Basic Books, Inc., 1961); R. A. Luke, Jr., and C. Seashore, "Generalizations on Research Related to Laboratory Training Design," *Human Relations Training News*, Winter, 1965–1966, p. i (4); L. E. Durham and J. R. Gibb, "A Bibliography of Research: 1947–1960," Part I of *Explorations* (National Training Laboratories, 1967); E. S. Knowles, "A Bibliography of Research: 1960–67," Part II of *Explorations* (National Training Laboratories, 1967); Alexander P. Hare and others, *Small Groups* (Alfred A. Knopf, Inc., 1955); Edgar H. Schein and Warren G. Bennis, *Personal and Organizational Change Through Group Methods* (John Wiley & Sons, Inc., 1965), esp. "Research on Laboratory Training Outcome," pp. 235 ff.; M. Argyle, "Methods of Studying Small Social Groups," *Brit. Journal of Psychology*, Vol. 43 (1952a), pp. 269–279.

7. H. E. Klein, "T-Groups: Talk, Training, or Therapy," *Science and Technology*, June, 1968; A. Winn, "Training Groups and Therapy Groups," *Human Relations Training News*, Fall, 1963, p. 7.

8. M. P. Jackson, "Their Brothers' Keeper—A Directory of Therapeutic Self-Help Groups, Intentional Communities, and Lay Training Centers," mimeographed (Department of Psychology, University of Illinois); John W. Drakeford, *Farewell to the Lonely Crowd* (Word Books, 1969); Walter O'Connell, "Psychotherapy for Everyman," *Journal of Existentialism*, Vol. VII, No. 25 (Fall, 1966); Hobart Mowrer, *The New Group Therapy* (D. Van Nostrand Company, Inc., 1964).

9. C. R. Mill, *Selections from Human Relations Training News* (National Training Laboratories, 1969); Warren G. Bennis and others (eds.), *The Planning of Change*, 2d ed.

(Holt, Rinehart & Winston, Inc., 1969).

10. For an introduction to humanistic psychology, see *Newsletter,* Association for Humanistic Psychology. Also see Abraham H. Maslow, *Toward a Psychology of Being* (D. Van Nostrand, Company, Inc., 1962), for an excellent bibliography; James F. T. Bugental, "The Third Force in Psychology," *Journal of Humanistic Psychology,* Vol. IV, No. 1 (1964), pp. 19–26; A. J. Sutich and M. A. Vich (eds.), *Readings in Humanistic Psychology* (The Macmillan Company, 1969); Frank T. Severin (ed.), *Humanistic Viewpoints in Psychology* (McGraw-Hill Book Company, 1965); James F. T. Bugental, *Challenges of Humanistic Psychology* (McGraw-Hill Book Company, 1967); Carl R. Rogers, *On Becoming a Person* (Houghton Mifflin Company, 1961); Carl R. Rogers and Barry Stevens, *Person to Person: The Problem of Being Human* (Real People Press, 1967); Abraham H. Maslow, *Motivation and Personality* (Harper & Brothers, 1954).

11. For an introduction to transactional analysis, see the following books by Eric Berne: *Transactional Analysis in Psychotherapy* (Grove Press, Inc., 1961); *The Structure and Dynamics of Organizations and Groups* (J. B. Lippincott Company, 1963); and *Games People Play* (Grove Press, Inc., 1964). Also, Thomas A. Harris, *I'm OK—You're OK* (Harper & Row, Publishers, Inc., 1969).

12. P. K. Greene, "Sensitivity Training: Fulfillment or Freakout?" *Catholic World,* Vol. 211 (April, 1970), pp. 18–21; Phyllis Chesler, "Playing Instant Joy in the Lonely Crowd," *The Village Voice,* Dec. 25. 1969; R. Cox, "The 'Being Real' Neurosis," *Century,* July 17, 1968.

13. Sam Keen, "The Soft Revolution," *The Christian Century,* Dec. 31, 1967, p. 1667; cf. Neil Postman and Charles Weingartner, *The Soft Revolution* (Dell Publishing Company, Inc., 1971).

14. Keen, "The Soft Revolution," p. 1667.

15. J. R. Gibb, "The Effects of Human Relations Training," in A. E. Bergin and S. L. Garfield (eds.), *Handbook of Psychotherapy and Behavior Change* (John Wiley & Sons, Inc., 1970), pp. 2114–2176.

16. Carl R. Rogers, *Carl Rogers on Encounter Groups*

(Harper & Row, Publishers, Inc., 1970), pp. 14 ff.; cf. B. W. Tuckman, "Developmental Sequence in Small Groups," *Psychological Bulletin,* Vol. 6 (1963), pp. 384–399; Betty Meador, "An Analysis of Process Movement in a Basic Encounter Group" (Ph.D. dissertation, United States International University, 1969).

17. See Arthur Burton (ed.), *Encounter* (Jossey-Bass, Inc., Publishers, 1969); Clark E. Moustakas, *Individuality and Encounter: A Brief Journey Into Loneliness and Sensitivity Groups* (Howard A. Doyle, Pub. Co., 1968); James F. T. Bugental and R. Tannenbaum, "Sensitivity Training and Being Motivation," *Journal of Humanistic Psychology,* Vol. III, No. 1 (1963), pp. 76–85.

18. Frederick Stoller, "Accelerated Interaction: A Time-limited Approach Based on the Brief Intensive Group," *International Journal of Group Psychotherapy,* Vol. XVIII, No. 2 (1968), pp. 220–258; George R. Bach, *Intensive Group Psychotherapy* (The Ronald Press Co., 1954).

19. William Carl Schutz, *Here Comes Everybody: Bodymind and Encounter Culture* (Harper & Row, Publishers, Inc., 1971), p. xiii.

20. Herbert Marcuse, *One Dimensional Man* (Beacon Press, Inc., 1966); Abbie Hoffman [Free], *Revolution for the Hell of It* (The Dial Press, Inc., 1968); Kenneth Keniston, *The Uncommitted: Alienated Youth in American Society* (Dell Publishing Company, Inc., 1967); cf. Theodore Roszak, *The Making of a Counter Culture* (Doubleday & Company, Inc., 1969). Admittedly there are many similarities between the counter culture and the encounter culture. We are not denying the similarities but are pointing instead to certain differences.

21. Charles Reich, *The Greening of America* (Random House, Inc., 1970).

Chapter One: A REPERTOIRE OF INTENSIVE
GROUP STRATEGIES

1. F. E. Fiedler, "The Psychological-Distance Dimension in Interpersonal Relations," *Journal of Personality*, Vol. 22 (1953b), pp. 142–150.

2. For further exploration of intensive group strategies, see Howard R. Lewis and Harold S. Streitfeld, *Growth Games* (Harcourt Brace Jovanovich, Inc., 1971); William Carl Schutz, *Joy* (Grove Press, Inc., 1967); W. G. Dyer, "An Inventory of Trainer Interventions," *Human Relations Training News*, Spring, 1963, p. 7 (1); J. William Pfeiffer and John E. Jones, *A Handbook of Structured Experiences for Human Relations Training* (University Associations Press, 1969); Bernard Gunther, *Sense Relaxation Below Your Mind* (Collier Books, 1968); Daniel I. Malamud and Solomon Machover, *Toward Self-Understanding: Group Techniques in Self-Confrontation* (Charles C Thomas, Publishers, 1965); Viola Spolin, *Improvisation for the Theater* (Northwestern University Press, 1963). I would not recommend Christopher Hills and Robert B. Stone, *Conduct Your Own Awareness Sessions* (The New American Library, Inc., 1971).

3. Martin Luther in E. M. Plass (ed.), *What Luther Says*, Vol. II (Concordia Publishing House, 1959), p. 872.

4. *Ibid.*, p. 871.

5. William Carl Schutz, *FIRO: A Three-Dimensional Theory of Interpersonal Behavior* (Rinehart & Company, Inc., 1958), pp. 13 ff.

6. H. Richard Niebuhr, *Radical Monotheism and Western Culture* (Harper & Brothers, 1960).

7. For further discussion of specific techniques in personal growth, see Herbert A. Otto and John Mann (eds.), *Ways of Growth* (The Viking Press, 1969); Roberto Assagioli, *Psychosynthesis* (Hobbs, Dorman & Company, Inc., 1965); Frederick M. Alexander, *The Resurrection of the Body*, ed. by Edward Maisel (University Books, 1969); Alexander Lowen, *Pleasure* (Coward-McCann, Inc., 1970); Ida Rolf, "Structural Integration," *Systematics*, Vol. I, No. 1 (June, 1963). I am

indebted to Stuart Gilbreath for the main outlines of the life cycle fantasy.

Chapter Two: THE NEW PIETISM

1. Carl R. Rogers, *Encounter Groups,* p. 1.

2. For further information concerning Jewish and Protestant pietism, see Albrecht Ritschl, *Geschichte des Pietismus,* 3 vols. (Bonn: A. Marcus, 1880–1886); A. Lang, *Puritanismus und Pietismus: Studien zu ihrer Entwicklung von M. Butzer bis zum Methodismus* (Neukirchen: K. Moers, 1941); C. D. Ensign, *Radical German Pietism* (Thesis, Boston University; Ann Arbor, Mich.: University Microfilms, 1955), and other works noted below.

3. A further attempt at corroboration of my hypothesis could be made by pursuing the biographies of persons who have shaped the encounter culture. See *Current Biography* (Yearbook, 1946–1968, published by The H. W. Wilson Company): Carl Rogers, Dec., 1962; Alan Watts, March, 1962; Martin Buber, July, 1965; Gordon Allport, Dec., 1967.

4. Dorwin Cartwright and A. F. Zander, "Origins of Group Dynamics," *Group Dynamics: Research and Theory,* 2d ed. (Row, Peterson & Company, 1960), pp. 3 ff.; Hubert Bonner, *Group Dynamics* (The Ronald Press Co., 1959), pp. 3 ff.; Kenneth D. Benne, "History of the T Group in the Laboratory Setting," in Bradford and others (eds.), *T-Group Theory and Laboratory Method,* pp. 80 ff.; Rudolph Dreikurs, "Early Experiments with Group Psychotherapy," *American Journal of Psychotherapy,* Vol. 13 (1959), pp. 219–255; H. L. Ansbacher, "The History of the Leaderless Group Discussion Technique," *Psychological Bulletin,* Vol. 48 (1951), pp. 383–391; Jacob L. Moreno, "The Viennese Origins of the Encounter Movement, Paving the Way for Existentialism, Group Psychotherapy and Psychodrama," *Group Psychotherapy,* Vol. XXII (1969), pp. 7–16.

5. For accounts of the historical background of the encounter group movement, see Jacob L. Moreno, *Die Gottheit als Komödiant* (Vienna: Anzengruber Verlag, 1911); *Einladung zu einer Begegnung* ("Invitation to an Encounter")

(Vienna: Anzengruber Verlag, 1914); "Die Gottheit als Autor," *Daimon* (Vienna: Anzengruber Verlag, 1918); *Das Testament des Vaters* (Berlin-Potsdam: Kiepenheuer Verlag, 1920); *Rede über den Augenblick* (Potsdam: Kiepenheuer Verlag, 1922); "Dramaturgy and Creaturgy," *Impromptu,* Vol. I, No. 1 (Jan., 1931), pp. 18–19; "The Philosophy of the Moment and the Spontaneity Theatre," *Sociometry,* Vol. IV (1941), pp. 205–226; *Who Shall Survive?* (Beacon House, Inc., 1953); Jacob L. Moreno (ed.), *Sociometry Reader* (The Free Press of Glencoe, Inc., 1960); Paul Johnson, *Psychology of Religion* (Abingdon Press, 1959), pp. 42 ff.; R. J. Corsini and L. J. Putzey, "Bibliography of Group Psychotherapy 1906–1956," *Psychodrama Group Psychotherapy Monograph,* No. 29, 1957; L. Cody Marsh, "Group Treatment as the Psychological Equivalent of the Revival," *Mental Hygiene,* Vol. 15 (1931), pp. 328–349.

6. Giovanni Pico della Mirandola, *Oration on the Dignity of Man* (Henry Regnery Company, Publishers, 1956); Carl Becker, *The Heavenly City of the Eighteenth Century Philosophers* (Yale University Press, 1950).

7. For information concerning frontier American pietism, see Warren G. Bennis and Philip E. Slater, *The Temporary Society* (Harper & Row, Publishers, Inc., 1968); William W. Sweet, *Methodism in American History* (Abingdon Press, 1933); Francis Asbury, *Journals,* 3 vols. (Lane and Scott, 1852); H. M. Muhlenberg, *The Journals of Henry Melchior Muhlenberg,* ed. and tr. by T. G. Tappert and J. W. Doberstein, 3 vols. (Muhlenberg Press, Publishers, 1942–1958).

8. Martin Schmidt and Wilhelm Jannasch (eds.), *Das Zeitalter des Pietismus* (Bremen: C. Schunemann, 1965); F. E. Stoeffler, *The Rise of Evangelical Pietism* (Leiden: E. J. Brill, 1965); John T. McNeill, *Modern Christian Movements* (The Westminster Press, 1954).

9. Gershom G. Scholem, *"Personality* Takes the Place of Doctrine," *Major Trends in Jewish Mysticism* (Schocken Books, Inc., 1941), p. 344; Louis I. Newman, *The Hasidic Anthology* (Bloch Publishing Company, Inc., 1944); Martin Buber, *Hasidism* (Philosophical Library, Inc., 1948); *Tales of the Hasidim,* 2 vols. (Schocken Books, Inc., 1948); Martin Buber (ed.), *Ten Rungs: Hasidic Sayings* (Schocken Books,

Inc., 1947); Solomon Schechter, "Hasidim and Hasidism," *Studies in Judaism*, Vol. 1 (Philadelphia, 1896), pp. 1 ff.; S. M. Dubnow, *History of the Jews in Russia and Poland*, tr. by I. Friendlander, Vol 1 (Philadelphia, 1916); Harry M. Rabinowicz, *A Guide to Hassidism* (Thomas Yoseloff, Inc., Publisher, 1960); Ernst Müller, *History of Jewish Mysticism* (Crown Publishers, 1946).

10. Paul Althaus, "Die Bekehrung in reformatorischer und pietistischer Sicht," *Neue Zeitschrift für systematische Theologie*, Vol. 1 (1959), pp. 3–25; W. G. Bodamer, "Some Features of Pietistic Biography," *Theologische Zeitschrift*, Vol. 17 (Nov.–Dec., 1961), pp. 435–437; S. G. Dimond, *The Psychology of the Methodist Revival* (Oxford, 1926).

11. Rogers, *Encounter Groups*, p. 34; cf. Moustakas, *Individuality and Encounter*, and R. Burke and W. Bennis, "Changes in Perception of Self and Others During Human Relations Training," *Human Relations*, Vol. II (1961), pp. 165–182.

12. William G. McLoughlin, "Pietism and the American Character," *American Quarterly*, Vol. 17, No. 2, Part 2 (Summer, 1965), pp. 163ff.

13. John Telford (ed.), *The Letters of the Rev. John Wesley*, 8 vols. (The Epworth Press, 1931); John Emory (ed.), *The Works of the Rev. John Wesley*, 7 vols. (Lane and Scott, 1850); Albert C. Outler (ed.), *John Wesley* (Oxford University Press, Inc., 1967); John S. Simon, *John Wesley and the Methodist Societies*, 2d ed. (The Epworth Press, 1937); A. W. Nagler, *Pietism and Methodism* (Smith & Lamar, 1918); Robert J. Treat, "Pastoral Care: According to Wesley," *Christian Advocate*, July 27, 1967, pp. 13 f.

14. Egon H. Gerdes, "Pietism, Classical and Modern; a Comparison of Two Representative Descriptions," *Concordia Theological Monthly*, Vol. 39 (April, 1968), pp. 257–268; A. C. Deeter, "Membership in the Body of Christ as Interpreted by Classical Pietism," *Brethren Life and Thought*, Vol. 9 (Autumn, 1964), pp. 18–49.

15. John R. Weinlick, *Count Zinzendorf* (Abingdon Press, 1956); O. Uttendörfer, *Zinzendorfs religiöse Grundgedanken* (Herrnhut, 1935); A. G. Spangenberg, *Idea fidei fratrum oder kurzer Begriff der Christlichen Lehre in den evange-*

lischen Brüdergemeinen (Barby, 1779); John Arndt, *True Christianity*, tr. and ed. by A. W. Boehm and C. F. Schaeffer (Smith, English & Co., 1868).

16. Horst Weigelt, "Interpretation of Pietism in the Research of Contemporary German Church Historians," *Church History*, Vol. 32, No. 2 (June, 1970), pp. 236–241; A. Tholuck, *Geschichte des Rationalismus* (Aalen: Scientia Verlag, 1970), originally published in 1865.

17. David Bakan, *Sigmund Freud and the Jewish Mystical Tradition* (Schocken Books, Inc., 1965), p. 26.

18. *Ibid.*, p. 33 (italics mine).

19. Alan W. Watts, *Psychotherapy East and West* (Pantheon Books, Inc., 1961); *This Is It* (Pantheon Books, Inc., 1960); F. C. S. Northrup, *The Meeting of East and West* (The Macmillan Company, 1946).

20. Leonidas Rosser, *Class Meetings* (Richmond, 1855), pp. 282–283. For further study of the encounter style of the Methodist class meeting, see John Atkinson, *The Class Leader* (Nelson and Phillips, 1875); S. W. Christophers, *Class Meetings in Relation to the Design and Success of Methodism* (London: Wesleyan Conference Office, 1873); T. Cordeux, *Class Book Containing Directions to Class Leaders* (London, 1820); S. Emerick, *Spiritual Renewal for Methodism* (Methodist Evangelistic Materials, 1958); P. D. Fitzgerald, *The Class Meeting* (Southern Methodist Publishing House, 1880); E. S. Janes, *Address to Class Leaders* (Carlton and Lanahan, 1868); John Miley, *Treatise on Class Meetings* (Poe & Hitchcock, 1866); James Wood, *Directions and Cautions Addressed to the Class Leaders* (London: Conference Office, 1809).

21. Schutz, *Here Comes Everybody*, pp. 149–154.

22. Emory (ed.), *Works of John Wesley*, Vol. V, pp. 184 f. (italics mine).

23. Charles Seashore, "What Is Sensitivity Training?" in National Training Laboratories, *Institute News and Reports*, Vol. II, No. 2 (April, 1968) (italics mine); cf. Abraham H. Maslow, "Notes on Unstructured Groups," *Human Relations Training News*, Fall, 1963, p. 7.

24. Emory (ed.), *Works of John Wesley*, Vol. V, pp. 184 f.

25. Schutz, quoted by Gustaitis in *Turning On*, p. 213.

26. John Wesley, *Journal*, Vol. II, p. 113; cf. John W.

Drakeford, *Integrity Therapy* (The Broadman Press, 1967).

27. Rogers, *Encounter Groups,* p. 7; cf. Samuel A. Culberg, *The Interpersonal Process of Self-Disclosure: It Takes Two to See One* (National Training Laboratories, 1968).

28. John Wesley, "Rules of the Bands," in Outler (ed.), *John Wesley,* p. 180.

29. "Objectives of Human Relations Training," 92 (National Training Laboratories, 1968) (italics mine).

30. Outler (ed.), *John Wesley,* p. 180.

31. Perls and others, *Gestalt Therapy,* p. 40.

32. Outler (ed.), *John Wesley,* p. 180.

33. Rosser, *Class Meetings,* p. 284.

34. Abraham H. Maslow, "Synanon and Eupsychia," *Journal of Humanistic Psychology,* Spring, 1967.

35. Outler (ed.), *John Wesley,* p. 180.

36. Schutz, *Here Comes Everybody,* p. 39.

37. Outler (ed.), *John Wesley,* p. 180.

38. Schutz, *Here Comes Everybody,* p. xvi.

39. Outler (ed.), *John Wesley,* p. 180.

40. Levitsky, "The Rules and Games of Gestalt Therapy," p. 10.

41. Newman, *The Hasidic Anthology,* p. 488.

42. Schutz, *Here Comes Everybody,* p. 63.

43. R. Newstead, *Advices to One who Meets in Class* (Lane and Sanford, 1843), pp. 17–18.

44. Perls, *Gestalt Therapy Verbatim.*

45. Newstead, *Advices,* p. 19.

46. Perls, quoted by Gustaitis, in *Turning On,* p. 49.

47. Rosser, *Class Meetings,* p. 286.

48. Schutz, *Here Comes Everybody,* p. 149.

49. Rosser, *Class Meetings,* p. 283.

50. Levitsky, "Rules and Games," p. 15.

51. Outler (ed.), *John Wesley,* p. 180.

52. Perls, quoted by James Simkin in "Introduction to Gestalt Therapy," mimeographed paper, p. 1.

53. Newstead, *Advices,* p. 18.

54. Schutz, *Joy,* p. 140.

55. Wesley, *Journal,* Vol. I, pp. 465 ff.

56. Lewis and Streitfeld, *Growth Games,* p. 18.

57. Rosser, *Class Meetings,* p. 287.

58. Rogers, *Encounter Groups*, p. 9.

59. Rosser, *Class Meetings*, p. 151.

60. Rogers, *Encounter Groups*, p. 8.

61. Rosser, *Class Meetings*, p. 283.

62. Rogers, *Encounter Groups*, p. 114.

63. Rosser, *Class Meetings*, p. 47, quoted from a source "prior to the act of conformity."

64. Rogers, *Encounter Groups*, p. 114.

65. "All Praise to Our Redeeming Lord," *The Methodist Hymnal* (1966), Hymn 301.

66. Telford (ed.), *Letters of John Wesley*, Vol. II, p. 8.

67. Schutz, *Here Comes Everybody*, p. 56.

68. "Jewish Revivalists" (A Discussion of the Maggidim, or Itinerant Preachers), *London Jewish World*, July 28, 1932, pp. 8–9; cf. Marsh, "Group Treatment as Psychological Equivalent"; Frederick Stoller, "The Long Weekend," *Psychology Today*, Dec., 1967, pp. 28–33; George R. Bach, "Marathon Group Dynamics III—Disjunctive Contacts," *Psychological Report*, Vol. 20 (1967), pp. 1163–1172; K. Lamott, "Marathon Therapy Is a Psychological Pressure Cooker," *The New York Times Magazine*, July 13, 1969.

69. Peter Cartwright, *Autobiography* (Abingdon, 1956); William G. McLoughlin, *The American Evangelicals, 1800–1900: An Anthology* (Harper & Row, Publishers, Inc., 1968), p. 46.

70. George R. Bach, "The Marathon Group: Intensive Practice of Intimate Interaction," *Psychological Report*, Vol. 18 (1966), pp. 995–1002.

71. Schutz, *Here Comes Everybody*, p. 127.

72. Charles G. Finney, "What a Revival of Religion Is," *Lectures on Revivals of Religion*, ed. by William G. McLoughlin (Harvard University Press, 1960).

73. Ruitenbeek, *The New Group Therapies*, pp. 158–159.

74. Jesse Lee, *A Short History of the Methodists in the United States of America* (Magill and Cline, 1810), p. 59.

75. Elizabeth Mintz, "Time-extended Marathon Groups," *Psychotherapy*, May, 1967.

76. Telford (ed.), *Letters of John Wesley*, Vol. II, p. 298.

77. Schutz, *Here Comes Everybody*, p. xv.

78. Cf. Wilhelm Reich, *The Function of the Orgasm* (Ban-

tam Books, Inc., 1967); Frederick S. Perls, *In and Out the Garbage Pail* (Real People Press, 1969); Kurt Lewin, *Resolving Social Conflicts*, ed. by Gertrud Lewin (Harper & Brothers, 1948); Martin Buber, *I and Thou*, 2d ed. (Charles Scribner's Sons, 1958); Erich Fromm, *Psychoanalysis and Religion* (Yale University Press, 1950).

79. Paul Robinson, *The Freudian Left* (Harper & Row, Publishers, Inc., 1969), p. 151.

80. Philip Jacob Spener, *Pia desideria,* tr. and ed. by T. G. Tappert (Fortress Press, 1964).

81. Robert H. Murray, *Group Movements Throughout the Ages* (Harper & Brothers, n.d.).

82. Cf. Philip Jacob Spener, *Theologische Bedenken,* 4 vols. (Halle: 1700–1702); J. Wallmann, *Philipp Jakob Spener und die Anfange des Pietismus* (Tübingen: J. C. B. Mohr [Paul Siebeck], 1970); Kurt Aland, *Spener-Studien* (Berlin: Walter de Gruyter, 1943).

83. John Wesley, *Wesley's Standard Sermons,* 3d ed., 2 vols., ed. by E. H. Sugden (Alec R. Allenson, Inc., 1921) Vol. II, pp. 126 ff.; Friedrich Schleiermacher, *The Christian Faith* (Edinburgh: T. & T. Clark, 1928), pp. 681 ff.

84. Cf. Carl R. Rogers, *Freedom to Learn* (Charles E. Merrill Publishing Company, 1969); Schutz, *Here Comes Everybody;* George B. Leonard, *Education and Ecstasy* (The Dial Press, Inc., 1968); Kenneth D. Benne and Bozidar Muntayn, *Human Relations in Curriculum Change* (The Dryden Press, Inc., 1951).

85. Hans-Martin Rotermund, *Orthodoxie und Pietismus* (Berlin: Evangelische Verlagsanstalt, 1960); cf. *Die Religion in Geschichte und Gegenwart,* Vol. IV (Tübingen: J. C. B. Mohr [Paul Siebeck], 1960), pp. 429–430.

86. Cf. Salomon Birnbaum, *Leben und Werke des Balschemm* (Berlin, 1920); John Wesley, *A Short View of the Difference Between the Moravian Brethren . . . and the Rev. Mr. John and Charles Wesley* (Bristol, 1748); John Wesley, *Queries Humbly Proposed to the Right Reverend and Right Honourable Count Zinzendorf* (London, 1755).

87. Cf. Martin Buber, *The Legend of the Baal-Shem,* tr. by Maurice Friedman (Harper & Brothers, 1955); Martin

Schmidt, *John Wesley: A Theological Biography*, tr. by Norman P. Goldhawk, Vol. I, 1703–1738 (Abingdon Press, 1963); Richard M. Cameron, *The Rise of Methodism: A Source Book* (Philosophical Library, Inc., 1954).

88. H. Watkin-Jones, "Two Oxford Movements: Wesley and Newman," *Hibbert Journal*, Oct., 1932; Outler (ed.), *John Wesley*, Introduction; Ronald H. Knox, *Enthusiasm* (Oxford University Press, Inc., 1961).

89. Keen, "The Soft Revolution," p. 1668.

90. Ernst Troeltsch, *The Social Teachings of the Christian Churches*, Vol. II (George Allen & Unwin, 1931); Timothy Smith, *Revivalism and Social Reform* (Harper & Row, Publishers, Inc., 1961); E. R. Taylor, *Methodism and Politics, 1791–1851* (Cambridge, 1935).

91. Sam Keen, "The Jesus Revolution," *Time*, June 21, 1971, pp. 56 ff.

92. F. W. Kantzenbach, *Orthodoxie und Pietismus* (Gütersloh: Gütersloher Verlagshaus Gerd Mohn, 1966).

93. Jay Stillson Judah, *The History and Philosophy of the Metaphysical Movements in America* (The Westminster Press, 1967), pp. 21 ff.; Donald B. Meyer, *The Positive Thinkers* (Doubleday & Company, Inc., 1965).

94. Marshall McLuhan and Quentin Fiore, *The Medium Is the Massage* (Bantam Books, Inc., 1967), p. 8.

95. *Ibid.*, pp. 68, 75.

96. For additional information concerning the media revolution, see Marshall McLuhan and Quentin Fiore, *War and Peace in the Global Village* (Bantam Books, Inc., 1968), pp. 4, 25; Marshall McLuhan, *The Gutenberg Galaxy: The Making of Typographic Man* (University of Toronto Press, 1962); *The Mechanical Bride: Folklore of Industrial Man* (Beacon Press, Inc., 1967); Marshall McLuhan, *Verbi-Voco-Visual Explorations* (Something Else Press, Inc., 1967); Harold A. Innis, *The Bias of Communication* (University of Toronto Press, 1951).

97. Burton (ed.), *Encounter;* A. Kirchhoff (ed.), *Theologie und Pietismus: Lebensberichte und Aufsätze* (Neukirchen: Neukirchener Verlag, 1961).

98. J. O. Bemesderfer, "Pietism: The Other Side," *Journal*

of Religious Thought, Vol. 25, No. 2 (1968–1969), pp. 29–38; E. Beyreuther, *Der geschichtliche Auftrag des Pietismus in der Gegenwart* (Stuttgart: Calwer Verlag, 1963).

Chapter Three: GROUP TRUST AND ULTIMATE TRUST

1. To explore further the human potential movement, see the following books: Herbert A. Otto (ed.), *Human Potentialities: The Challenge and the Promise* (Warren H. Green, Inc., 1968); *Explorations in Human Potentialities* (Charles C Thomas, Publishers, 1966); Herbert A. Otto, *Guide to Developing Your Potential* (Charles Scribner's Sons, 1967); Gardner Murphy, *Human Potentialities* (Basic Books, Inc., Publishers, 1958); Howard, *Please Touch;* Miller, *Hot Spring;* Gustaitis, *Turning On.*

2. Cf. W. V. Ault, *A Theological Context for a Theory of Group Dynamics* (Dissertation, University of Chicago; University Microfilms, 1962); Kenneth Scott Latourette, *A History of Christianity* (Harper & Brothers, 1953), pp. 1063 ff.

3. The following are basic resources for a theology of secularization: Friedrich Gogarten, *Verhängnis und Hoffnung der Neuzeit* (Stuttgart: Friedrich Vorwerk Verlag, 1953); *Jesus Christus Wende der Welt: Grundfragen der Christologie* (Tübingen: J. C. B. Mohr [Paul Siebeck], 1966); Arend Theodoor van Leeuwen, " 'Christianization' and Secularization," *Christianity in World History* (Charles Scribner's Sons, 1964), pp. 411 ff., also pp. 331 ff.; Larry Shiner, *The Secularization of History* (Abingdon Press, 1966); Johannes Baptist Metz, *Zur Theologie der Welt* (Mainz: Matthias-Grünewald-Verlag, 1968); Carl Michalson, *Worldly Theology* (Charles Scribner's Sons, 1967); Robert L. Richard, *Secularization Theology* (Herder & Herder, Inc., 1967); Harvey Cox, *The Secular City* (The Macmillan Company, 1965); Joachim Friese, *Die Säkularisierte Welt* (Frankfurt: Schulte-Bulmke, 1967).

4. Martin Heidegger, *Being and Time,* tr. by John Macquarrie and Edward Robinson (SCM Press, Ltd., 1962); James F. T. Bugental, *The Search for Authenticity* (Holt,

Rinehart & Winston, Inc., 1965); Viktor E. Frankl, *Man's Search for Meaning* (Beacon Press, Inc., 1963).

5. Cf. Jack Gibb, "Climate for Trust Formation," in Bradford and others (eds.), *T-Group Theory and Laboratory Method;* Everett L. Shostrom, "Trusting Yourself in the Here and Now," *Man, the Manipulator* (Abingdon Press, 1967), pp. 52 ff.; Thomas Hora, "Transcendence and Healing," *Journal of Existential Psychiatry,* Vol. I (1961), pp. 501–511; R. D. Laing, "The Existential-Phenomenological Foundations for a Science of Persons," *The Divided Self* (Penguin Books, Inc., 1965), pp. 17 ff.

6. J. L. Loomis, "Communication, the Development of Trust and Cooperative Behavior," *Human Relations,* Vol. XII (1959), pp. 305–315.

7. Thomas Oden, *The Structure of Awareness* (Abingdon Press, 1968), Part II.

8. Cf. Emil Brunner, *Truth as Encounter* (The Westminster Press, 1964); Paul Tillich, *The Courage to Be* (Yale University Press, 1952); Jürgen Moltmann, *Theology of Hope* (Harper & Row, Publishers, Inc., 1967); James M. Robinson and John B. Cobb, Jr. (eds.), New Frontiers in Theology, Vol. III: *Theology as History* (Harper & Row, Publishers, Inc., 1967); cf. Martin Buber, *Between Man and Man* (Beacon Press, Inc., 1961).

9. Julius Fast, *Body Language* (M. Evans & Company, Inc., 1970); W. B. Cannon, *Wisdom of the Body* (W. W. Norton & Company, Inc., 1932); Edward T. Hall, *The Silent Language* (Fawcett Publications, Inc., 1970); Albert E. Scheflen, "The Significance of Posture in Communication Systems," *Psychiatry,* Vol. 27 (1964), pp. 316–331; Seymour Fisher and Sidney E. Cleveland, *Body Image and Personality* 2d rev. ed. (Dover Publications, Inc., 1968); Alexander Lowen, *Betrayal of the Body* (The Macmillan Company, 1967); Albert Pesso, *Movement in Psychotherapy: Psychomotor Techniques and Training* (New York University Press, 1969); Charles Darwin, *The Expression of the Emotions in Man and Animals* (The University of Chicago Press, 1965); Desmond Morris, *The Naked Ape* (Dell Publishing Company, Inc., 1967); Robert Ardrey, *The Territorial Imperative* (Dell Publishing Company, Inc., 1966).

10. Harvey Cox, *The Feast of Fools: A Theological Essay on Festivity and Fantasy* (Harvard University Press, 1969); Jacques Sarano, *The Meaning of the Body*, tr. by James H. Farley (The Westminster Press, 1966), pp. 115 ff.; Sam Keen, *To a Dancing God* (Harper & Row, Publishers, Inc., 1970).

11. *The Book of Worship for Church and Home* (The Methodist Publishing House, 1952), p. 380.

12. Wilhelm Reich, *Character-Analysis* (Noonday Press, 1949), pp. 360 ff.

13. Marshall McLuhan, *The Gutenberg Galaxy;* Walter Ong, *The Presence of the Word* (Simon & Schuster, Inc., Publishers, 1970).

14. Josef Pieper, *In Tune with the World: A Theory of Festivity* (Harcourt, Brace & World, Inc., 1965); Hugo Rahner, *Man at Play*, tr. by Brian Battershaw and Edward Quinn (Herder & Herder, Inc., 1967); Johan Huizinga, *Homo Ludens: A Study of the Play-Element in Culture* (Beacon Press, Inc., 1955); Cox, *Feast of Fools;* David L. Miller, *Gods and Games* (The World Publishing Company, 1969); Robert E. Neale, *In Praise of Play* (Harper & Row, Publishers, Inc., 1969); Karl Barth, *Church Dogmatics*, Vol. III, Part 4, ed. by G. W. Bromiley and T. F. Torrance (Edinburgh: T. & T. Clark, 1961), Section 53, "The Holy Day."

15. William James, *The Varieties of Religious Experience* (Modern Library, Inc., 1942); Meyer, *The Positive Thinkers.*

16. Carl R. Rogers, "A Theory of Therapy, Personality and Interpersonal Relationships," in Sigmund Koch (ed.), *Psychology: A Study of a Science*, Vol. III (McGraw-Hill Book Co., Inc., 1959); Karen Horney, *Neurosis and Human Growth* (W. W. Norton & Company, Inc., 1951); Maslow, *Toward a Psychology of Being.*

17. Herbert Marcuse, *Eros and Civilization* (Beacon Press, Inc., 1956).

18. R. N. Flew, *The Idea of Perfection in Christian Theology* (Oxford University Press, 1934).

19. James V. Clark, "Toward a Theory and Practice of Religious Experiencing," in James F. T. Bugental (ed.), *The Challenge for Humanistic Psychology* (McGraw-Hill Book Co., Inc., 1966).

20. Rogers, *Freedom to Learn.*

21. Neil Postman and Charles Weingartner, *Teaching as a Subversive Activity* (The Dial Press, Inc., 1969); George Leonard, *Education and Ecstasy;* Eva Schindler Rainman, "Telling Is Not Teaching," (American Dietetic Association, Chicago: The Association, Aug., 1960).

22. Cf. my essay "Optimal Conditions for Learning—Toward a Clarification of the Learning Contract," *Religious Education,* March–April, 1972.

Chapter Four: INCONSISTENCIES AND MISCALCULATIONS OF THE MOVEMENT

1. John Steinbacher, *The Child Seducers* (Educator Publications, Dec., 1970), pp. 150–186; J. D. Black, "Opinion: Encounter Groups," *Mademoiselle,* Vol. 71, No. 33 (May, 1970); Andrew M. Greeley, *Come Blow Your Mind with Me* (Doubleday & Company, Inc., 1971); Greene, "Sensitivity Training"; Chesler, "Playing Instant Joy," Cox, "The 'Being Real' Neurosis."

2. Ruitenbeek, *The New Group Therapies,* p. 233.

3. Quoted by Gustaitis in *Turning On,* p. 38.

4. Rollo May, *Love and Will* (W. W. Norton & Company, Inc., 1969).

5. D. H. Lawrence, *The Complete Poems of D. H. Lawrence,* collected and ed. by Vivian de Sola Pinto and Warren Roberts, 2 vols. (The Viking Press, Inc., 1964); D. H. Lawrence, *The Later D. H. Lawrence,* ed. by William Y. Tindall (Alfred A. Knopf, Inc., 1959).

6. Sam Keen, "My New Carnality," *Psychology Today,* Oct., 1970; "Sing the Body Electric," *Psychology Today;* Nikos Kazantzakis, *Zorba the Greek* (Simon & Schuster, Inc., 1965); Norman O. Brown, *Love's Body* (Random House, Inc., 1966).

7. Alan W. Watts, *The Joyous Cosmology: Adventures in the Chemistry of Consciousness* (Pantheon Books, Inc., 1962), foreword by Timothy Leary and Richard Alpert; Aldous Huxley, *The Doors of Perception and Heaven and Hell* (Harper & Row, Publishers, Inc., 1956).

8. Willis W. Harman, "The Psychedelic Experience," in Otto and Mann (eds.), *Ways of Growth;* Charles T. Tart, *Altered States of Consciousness* (John Wiley & Sons, Inc., 1969).

9. Schutz, *Here Comes Everybody,* p. 57.

10. Quoted by Gustaitis in *Turning On,* p. 92.

11. Paul Bindrim, "Nudity as a Quick Grab for Intimacy in Group Therapy," *Psychology Today,* Vol. III, No. 1 (June, 1969); Paul Bindrim, "A Report on a Nude Marathon," *Psychotherapy,* Vol. V, No. 3 (Fall, 1968); Alexander Lowen, "In Defense of Modesty," *The Journal of Sex Research,* Vol. I, IV, No. 1 (Feb., 1968), p. 52.

12. Keen, "The Soft Revolution," p. 1669.

13. *Medical World News,* March 27, 1970.

14. See John C. Cooper, *Religion in the Age of Aquarius* (The Westminster Press, 1971); Greeley, *Come Blow Your Mind with Me;* Chad Walsh, *God at Large* (The Seabury Press, 1971); Mayananda, *The Tarot for Today* (Zeus Press, 1968).

15. Schutz, *Here Comes Everybody,* p. 60.

16. Keen, "The Soft Revolution," p. 1668.

17. Mircea Eliade, *Cosmos and History* (Harper & Brothers, 1959); *The Sacred and the Profane* (Harper & Row, Publishers, Inc., 1961); Gerardus van der Leeuw, *Sacred and Profane Beauty: The Holy in Art* (Holt, Rinehart & Winston, Inc., 1963); *Religion in Essence and Manifestation* (Harper & Row, Publishers, Inc., 1963).

18. Paul Bindrim, "Facilitating Peak Experiences," in Otto and Mann (eds.), *Ways of Growth,* pp. 115 ff.

19. Quoted by Keen in "The Soft Revolution," p. 1668.

20. D. W. Brown, "The Problem of Subjectivism in Pietism: A Redefinition with Special Reference to the Theology of P. J. Spener and A. H. Francke" (Dissertation, Garrett Theological Seminary, 1962).

21. Cf. esp. Thomas C. Oden, *Radical Obedience* (The Westminster Press, 1964), pp. 58 ff., 61, 80 ff.

22. Rudolf Bultmann, "New Testament and Mythology," in H. W. Bartsch (ed.), *Kerygma and Myth* (SCM Press, Ltd., 1957), pp. 22 ff. Cf. Thomas C. Oden, *Contemporary*

Theology and Psychotherapy (The Westminster Press, 1967), pp. 112 ff.

23. Bultmann, "New Testament and Mythology," p. 26.

24. Eric Hoffer, *The Ordeal of Change* (Harper & Row, Publishers, Inc., 1963).

25. For information concerning this tradition, see Norman Cohn, *The Pursuit of the Millennium: Revolutionary Messianism in Medieval and Reformation Europe and Its Bearing on Modern Totalitarian Movements*, 2d ed. (Harper & Row, Publishers, Inc., 1961); Lewis Mumford, *The Story of Utopias* (The Viking Press, Inc., Publishers, 1962); Gerald Feinberg, "A Possible Goal—the Extension of Consciousness," *The Prometheus Project: Mankind's Search for Long-Range Goals* (Doubleday & Company, Inc., 1969), pp. 166 ff.; Robert Boguslaw, *The New Utopians: A Study of System Design and Social Change* (Prentice-Hall, Inc., 1965); Ernst Bloch, *Das Prinzip Hoffnung*, 3 vols. (Berlin: Aufbau-Verlag, 1959–1960); Martin Buber, *Pathways in Utopia* (London: Routledge & Kegan Paul, Ltd., 1949); B. F. Skinner, *Walden Two* (The Macmillan Company, 1948); Paul Goodman, *Utopian Essays and Practical Proposals* (Random House, Inc., 1964); Judith N. Shklar, *After Utopia: The Decline of Political Faith* (Princeton University Press, 1957); Eric Hoffer, *The True Believer* (The New American Library of World Literature, Inc., 1951).

Chapter Five: ENCOUNTER AND CELEBRATION

1. Similar issues were discussed in the 1950's, but with less radical alternatives. See P. Anderson, "Group Dynamics in a Local Church," *Pastoral Psychology*, Jan., 1953; John L. Casteel (ed.), *Spiritual Renewal Through Personal Groups* (Association Press, 1957); Ross Snyder, "Group Dynamics in the Life of the Church," *Religious Education*, Nov., 1951; Harold W. Freer and F. B. Hall, *Two or Three Together* (Harper & Brothers, 1954); Paul F. Douglass, *The Group Workshop Way in the Church* (Association Press, 1956); *Small Groups* (Pamphlet, Division of Evangelism, Presbyterian

Church U.S.A., n.d.). For more recent discussions, see William W. Meisner, S.J., *Group Dynamics in the Religious Life* (University of Notre Dame Press, 1965); Clyde Reid, *Groups Alive—Church Alive* (Harper & Row, Publishers, Inc., 1969); Robert C. Leslie, *Sharing Groups in the Church* (Abingdon Press, 1970).

2. G. Hearn, "Leadership and the Spatial Factor in Small Groups," *Journal of Abnormal Social Psychology*, 54, 2, 1957.

3. Robert R. Blake and Jane Mouton, *The Managerial Grid* (Gulf Publishing Company, 1964); Ralph K. White and Ronald Lippitt, *Autocracy and Democracy* (Harper & Brothers, 1960).

4. Eugène L. Backman, *Religious Dances in the Christian Church and in Popular Medicine* (Allen & Unwin, 1952); Ong, *The Presence of the Word.*

5. B. M. Bass and S. Klubeck, "Effects of Seating Arrangement on Leaderless Group Discussions," *Journal of Abnormal Social Psychology*, Vol. 47 (1952), pp. 724–727; Jurgen Ruesch and Wheldon Kees, *Nonverbal Communication* (University of California Press, 1956).

6. William Birmingham, "The Eroticization of Liturgy," *Continuum*, Winter, 1968; Margaret Fisk Taylor, *A Time to Dance* (United Church Press, 1967); Marshall McLuhan, *Understanding Media: The Extensions of Man* (McGraw-Hill Book Co., Inc., 1965).

7. Edgar Z. Friedenberg, *The Vanishing Adolescent* (Dell Publishing Company, 1962); Paul Goodman, *Growing Up Absurd* (Random House, Inc., 1960); Lewis Yablonsky, *The Hippie Trip* (Pegasus, 1968).

8. A. Daigon and R. T. LaConte, *Dig U.S.A.* (Bantam Books, Inc., 1970); *The Harrad Letters to Robert H. Rimmer* (The New American Library of World Literature, Inc., 1969).

9. R. Strand, "White Collar Hippies: Solid Citizens Turning On," *Minnesota Sunday Tribune*, Aug. 20, 1967; Ross Snyder, *Young People and Their Culture* (Abingdon Press, 1969), pp. 27 ff., 133 ff.

10. Sam Keen, *Apology for Wonder* (Harper & Row, Publishers, Inc., 1969), pp. 152 ff.; Wilhelm Reich, *The Sexual Revolution*, 4th ed. (Farrar, Straus & Giroux, Inc., 1969).

11. For an attempt to pursue this issue further, see Thomas

C. Oden, *Beyond Revolution: A Response to the Underground Church* (The Westminster Press, 1970).

12. Sam Keen, "The Importance of Being Carnal—Notes for a Visceral Theology," *To a Dancing God*, p. 141; Cox, "A Theology of Juxtaposition," *The Feast of Fools*, pp. 131 ff.; Ross Snyder, *On Becoming Human* (Abingdon Press, 1967); Reuel L. Howe, *The Miracle of Dialogue* (The Seabury Press, 1963).

13. Dietrich Bonhoeffer, *Prisoner for God* (The Macmillan Company, 1957), p. 164.

14. *Ibid.*, p. 140.

15. James M. Robinson and John B. Cobb, Jr. (eds.), New Frontiers in Theology, Vol. II: *The New Hermeneutic* (Harper & Row, Publishers, Inc., 1964).